The magic of Galicia

About the author

Knud Hammerschmidt
Born in Germany in 1963,
married, living in Munich.
Traveling is a passion to him,
the best way to meet new friends,
to discover, to learn and to experience.
Since this first Camino in 2012, he walked
the Caminho Portuguese in 2013 and is
already in anticipation of all the other ways
to Santiago. Presumably in the month of
May he can be found along the way.
When he is not traveling, he likes to cook, to
surf, to cross town on a skateboard and
enjoy the company of good friends in a
Munich beer garden.
Among (mostly German but some of APOC
too) pilgrims with a strong affinity to social
networks, he is not unknown and may even
be considered notorious.
http://facebook.com/knudthedude

"Time is an illusion. Lunchtime doubly so."
Douglas Adams

Knud Hammerschmidt

Dude looks like a Pilgrim

El Camino for Beginners
The Saint James Way from Leon to Santiago

This book is meant as a declaration of love to the Camino,
as a guidebook and maybe an inspiration and last but
not least as, hopefully, an amusement.

"One´s destination is never a place,
  but a new way of seeing things."
  Henry Miller

"Not all those who wander are lost."
  J.R.R. Tolkien

"Wandering re-establishes the original harmony
  which once existed between man and universe."
  Anatole France

"So throw off the bowlines, sail away from the safe
harbour. Catch the wind in your sails.
Explore. Dream. Discover."
  Mark Twain

1st Edition; 2014
Copyright: Knud Hammerschmidt
Translated from German.
Original title "Ohne Schmerz kein Halleluja"
Published byBoD-Books on Demand, Norderstedt 2012
Translation by Knud Hammerschmidt
Editor: Heather Nygren
ISBN: 978-3-7386-0828-1

For my grandparents and everybody
who taught me lessons in life.

Thanks to my pilgrim buddy Tom and
thanks to all the cool and lovely people
I met.

"You are stardust. You are golden." *

* Thanks to Joni Mitchell for the quote.

Dude looks like a pilgrim.

Good idea, caused by a stupid reason

There are as many reasons to walk the St. James way as there are people that walk it. And almost everybody is able to walk the way. As long as one is halfway healthy it is not even a question of age.

Until April 2012, I did not have the slightest inclination to walk on my own feet for a few hundred kilometers through the north of Spain. Of course, I knew about the Camino. But there was no reason for me to do it. I had found my spiritual way in life a long time ago. I was able to carry the weights and burdens of life and I was not that much into sports.

And then, out of nowhere, as malicious as a Disney witch, my midlife crisis lingered round the corner and flashed me an evil grin. My inner Peter Pan screamed like the first victim in a teenage slasher movie. The little scumbag took the chance to remind me of the fact that there was less than one year until I'd reach the magic frontier called FIFTY. I tried to calm him down with a drink and the declaration that fifty is the new thirty-nine. No way, José. My inner Peter

Pan wanted some adventure. He told me that it is not hip to be square. He babbled something about backpacks and reminded me of Greece, Indonesia, Paris, Istanbul, Amsterdam and New Orleans. And one of my buddies, Reinhard, who already did the way twice, backed him up and didn't stop telling me how wonderful the Camino de Santiago is. It took me a few drinks to calm my inner voice, and then I surrendered. Four weeks later, I'm sitting at the gate of Munich airport, waiting for my flight to Oviedo /Asturias with two weeks time and 320 kilometers to walk. From Leon to Santiago de Compostela.

Why Leon – Santiago?

Of course there are some other possibilities to walk along the way. Some have the luck of having enough time to walk the whole 790 kilometres. Some split the stages over a few years. And some take one of the shorter routes to Santiago, like the Camino Portuguese or the Camino Primitivo, which can be done in an average of two weeks. I, like many others, had the intention to reach Santiago on my first Camino. It may well be that the way is the destination, but every pilgrim wants to reach Santiago de

Compostela. Having followed ancient trails, to a place that has been a destination of desire for so many over more than thousand years. To catch the special spirit. To have arrived together with others one has met along the way.

Since I did not know if I would repeat that kind of walk, and considering the fact that I only had two weeks time, starting at Leon became my choice. Of course another starting point, like Ponferrada, Sarria or Portomarin is possible too, but a normal human being needs about 10 days to get into the real pilgrims groove.

Great Expectations

What to expect? It depends on you. It could be one of the best experiences in your entire life, maybe just a good time, or possibly tears and pain.

The best scenario is to expect nothing and to be prepared for everything. It does not matter if you do the way for spiritual or religious reasons, because of a sportive or adventurous challenge or just for fun. Whatever you experience, the way will change you.

You will go beyond your known limits. You will meet people from all over the planet, and you are going to know them in a way you never will in your daily life, because you and they all share the same exceptional circumstances. You will experience extremes, hospitality, friendship, amiability, love and last but not least yourself. Absolute strangers might tell you their deepest thoughts, you will have a fantastic time, you will swear and curse, you will be proud of yourself and others, you will sympathize, laugh, savour, drink and enjoy. And when you are back, at home, a part of you will remain there on the Camino de Santiago.

Remember: it is your way. "The Way" is a good movie, not more, not less. Something like "the way" doesn't exist. It is always your way. So walk with cheer, an open mind and without expectations – and everything might happen.

Some Basics, Facts and some Experiences

The Credential and the Compostela...

...is something like the alpha and the omega for a pilgrim. The pilgrimage starts with the "credencial", the certificate that proves you are a pilgrim; it is your pilgrims' passport and the precondition to stay at the pilgrims' albergues. The credential is stamped at the albergues and, if you like to, at many other places along the way, like bars and restaurants, museums and churches. The stamped credential (Spanish: stamps = sellos) is the proof for the pilgrims office at Santiago, that you have walked the way or done it by bicycle. As a walking pilgrim the minimal distance you must have done is 100 kilometres and as a biker you must have done 200 kilometres to receive the Compostela.

One stamp a day proves your pilgrimage to the Oficina de Peregrinos at Santiago.

If you only do the last 100 / 200 kilometres you must verify the pilgrimage by two stamps a day. The Compostela is the diploma that is given to the pilgrims to honour them and their merit. It is written in Latin, even your name will be written in a latin version.

In many Catholic countries, the Compostela is even added to one's résumé. During an application submission, the Compostela might be an advantage in competition. Together with a colorful and fully stamped credential, the Compostela is a very ornamental memory. Where do you get a credential? Along the way in every important place (like Saint Jean Pied de Port, Roncevalles, Pamplona) and every bigger place like Logrono, Leon or Ponferrada. And of course you can order it by mail at the associations and fraternities of Saint James all over the world. A choice of them is to be found in the chapter *"Links and Websites"*.

The Albergues

There are different kinds of albergues along the way. Some are lead by institutions, some by municipalities and some by private owners. They are often cognizable as churchly (paroquial) or local (municipal). In Galicia is another kind of albergue to be found. They are run by the Galician provincial government and have the label "Xunta Gallega". The price for a bunk bed in one of the above mentioned albergues can be a modest donation (mostly churchly albergues with almost no comfort) between five to eight Euros. Private Albergues offer their beds and rooms between nine and fifteen Euros. I have learned to prefer the private ones if I have the choice. They are often much more tidy and offer better service and facilities.

Some Albergues offer the option to use their kitchen; many have facilities to do laundry and some private ones even offer a laundry service. Every year, there are more new hostels along the way. Many of them are not

11

even mentioned in the guidebooks. New albergues are often promoted along the way by locals that distribute flyers. Computer terminals and Wi-Fi are meanwhile a standard on Saint James way. In interesting, bigger cities, I truly recommend not to stay in an Albergue. Why? Albergues usually close their doors about ten o'clock in the night. If you are having a good time in Leon, for example, enjoying the innumerable Tapas bars and the fantastic nightlife – you don't want to be the one that has to leave the party first. Sometimes a cheap little hotel is a better choice.

If you need some more comfort and want to make a reservation in advance in a neat little guesthouse or hotel, I can recommend the website: http://www.yourspainhostel.com. The website is very helpful if you are looking for a nice hotel at Santiago, too.

Food and Nutrition

The Spanish cuisine is a bit different from others, and if your stomach is not used to grease and lard, you may have a few digestion problems. Furthermore, if you are from the US, please consider the fact that food in the States is produced differently than European food. The European community laws about food are more strict and do not allow many additives that are used in the US. This might cause irritations too. Please remember, that the chances to get a food poisoning are very low. If you are used to organic grown food the risk is even lower. Many so called food-poisonings are simply an indigestion caused by unfamiliar food. Boost your system! You can get used to a diet that's different than at home.

Have some hot and spicy Mexican, Indian or Thai-food, try some heavy and greasy soul food, have a few bowls of gumbo and some jambalaya before you come to Spain and it will be a lot easier. Besides it will be yummy.

Vegetarians are meanwhile an accepted form of life in Spain. But the average Spaniard still believes that chicken is some kind of vegetable. If you are not too strict about your vegetarian diet you can ignore that a vegetable soup might be prepared with a poultry broth. Every region in Spain has its own specialties, although some dishes are to be found everywhere. The Spanish cuisine is not very spicy; it is rural and not very sophisticated. Its good taste comes from the quality of the basic materials. So if you give other dishes than steak, fries, bocadillo and hamburguesa a chance, you might be surprised. Vegans: please be strong. I am afraid you have to prepare your food by yourself. There may be some vegan living persons in Spain, but the Camino does not provide this kind of diet actually.

Infrastructure Along the Way

I guess I already mentioned it: El Camino is not the Appalachian Trail and not a trip through the black heart of Africa. Every few kilometres you will pass through a village, a hamlet or a town. There are some parts of the way that are very rural. (Behind Astorga and Ponferrada, for example). This means, that you will find albergues, hostels, small shops, bars and restaurants without problems. But it can take a few days until you find the next ATM or a shop that sells sun lotion.

Triacastela for example has a bank and a cash dispenser, but the dispenser is only available during the business hours of the bank.

Remember to talk to your bank before you arrive in Spain. Let them explain how to be prepared for the financial differences in Europe; ex: European ATM´s seem to be a bit different from American ones. I have seen some frustrated comments on facebook sites of American Pilgrims on the Camino

(APOC) about the European ATM´s. While travelling I always carry two credit cards with me. One in case of need, and one to draw money from the ATM. A PIN code is always required!

The Stages

Not everybody walking the way is a sporting ace. Actually most are the opposite. There are a few superheroes that walk in average 40 – 50 kilometres a day. This is very impressive. But there are better ways of being awesome. Most of us are more like Bruce Banner than like the Hulk. A healthy average of 20 – 30 kilometres a day is possible and offers you enough time to enjoy the walk and the surroundings.
Just listen to your body. Work with it, not against it. There is a difference between improvements and forcing one's body to things it is not used to. After you have done your way, you will have lost a few pounds anyway and will have gained some muscles in your legs and derriere. With an average speed of 4 or 5 kilometres per hour, a short hourly rest of 10 minutes and a longer break around noon, you will have made 25 kilometres very comfortably in seven or

eight hours. The first three days will be tough and then it gets easier.

Do not walk with the horde, and do not follow exactly the recommended stages in your guidebook. There are many other, not so popular but remarkable places along the way that will please you. A good side effect is: you don't need to join the bed race!

Maps and Guidebooks

One of the most common issues is the question of maps. Well, if you are the kind of person that likes a graphic presentation, get yourself a map. On the way you are not often going to use it. I promise. A famous guidebook is the "Brierley". There are other popular books too, and all are to be found in bookstores and of course online.

This is Not a Packing List.

In the following chapters you will find advice and suggestions about clothing, shoes and equipment, but it is not a packing list as such. On the one hand, I don't believe in packing lists. On the other one, it is part of the fun to make choices and to get all your stuff together instead of following a list.

Outfit, Backpack and sleeping bag

Of most importance is a pair of good and comfortable hiking boots. The popular keen sandals or trainers might appear inviting, but they won't make you happy on a long distance walk. Trail running shoes can be good for the feet but they don't protect the ankles. First of all your feet need protection and balance. The walking boots will be like your home, your car, your safety zone for the next few weeks. You need to rely on them. You cannot rely on footwear that allows humidity and pebbles to intrude, and that does not support your ankles. Buy your shoes in the afternoon, wear thick socks and buy them one or two sizes bigger than you usually wear. Trust me: your feet will be swollen and you will be thankful for every inch of comfort in your shoes. The second thing of great importance for your walk will be your socks. Don't be closefisted on shoes and socks. You will be thankful for a good high-tech quality. No tennis-socks or anything like that. There is a reason why the hiking stockings and socks are marked in their pattern with the letters R and L, which are meant to remind you which the right and left sock are. That does not mean that the sock-manufacturers implicit that customers are clumsy. It shall help to you avoid blisters by not confusing right and left sock. Because of the fact that you are going to carry your personal belongings with you for a few weeks the magic word is "weight". Which means anything you carry should be of light weight. The clothes you are going to wear should be made of microfibers or similar materials that are quick drying. I usually have 3 tank tops, 2 long sleeves, 3 sets of microfiber underwear, 4 pairs of walking socks, 2 microfiber cargo-pants and 1 cheap cagoule with me. The lighter the material is - the better for you. I have two towels of different sizes, both made of microfiber. On the belt on my hips, I carry a half liter water bottle and a small pack that contains a guide, my pilgrims-credential, maybe a moleskin notebook and some small items I need on the way. The sleeping bag should be light and suitable for sleeping outdoors too. Even if you are not planning to sleep outdoors. The albergues can be cold until the early summer, the buildings are often not well heated and when in the mountains you will be thankful for a snugly sleeping bag. I suggest a silk inlet for your sleeping bag. It is more comfortable even if the nights are warm and are a protection against bed bugs too. A pair of (light!) sandals or flip flops is useful for the bathrooms, and in the evening hours at the albergue.

And now we have to put all the above-mentioned things into a backpack! Believe it or not, but a pack with 30 up to 50 liters is sufficient. As long as it is waterproof and fits comfortably to your shoulders, chest and hips everything is fine. I never carry more than 7 or 8 kilograms on my back.

Accessory, Equipment and Gadgets

Advice about medicine and hygienic items like shower gel and shampoo in general: It is sufficient to take one small bottle of each article with you. You can purchase anything on the way. Spain is absolutely civilized and in every drugstore, pharmacy and supermarket, you can fill up your stock, so do not carry too much with you and have faith in modern logistics. A pilgrim's medicine chest should contain resolvable magnesium pellets and ascorbic acid as an addition to your drinking water. It helps to avoid muscular cramps. Add some aspirin, which is a good prophylaxis against thrombosis and of course mother's little helper against the aftermath of Spanish wine, and a medicine of your choice against diarrhea. Ibuprofen is the favorite pilgrims' drug, as it is a perfect painkiller and can be bought in Spain very cheaply as highly concentrated as IBU 600. Next, your personal drugstore should contain a mixed selection of plasters and patches for blisters, a disinfection spray for wounds, some gauze bandage and, most importantly, ointment for your feet. I usually have two ointments with me. A gel with mint to cool down my feet and a lotion that contains 10 – 20% urea which softens and soothes the feet after a long day walking.

Against the eventuality of chafing, I suggest Vaseline or something similar. Your bum will be grateful. The SPF of your lotion should be minimum of 30. All the way the sun will be shining from the left, so this side needs more protection, in the evening your skin will be thankful for after sun lotion or aloe vera lotion.

Another helpful item for protection against any kind of weather is a bandana, which can be used as a headscarf, a shawl or a headband. In case you still have some space in your luggage, take a hat with you.

What Else?

Very helpful items are: 2 or 3 safety pins, 2 needles (in case you need to puncture a blister) 2 meters of cord, 4 clothespins, a miniature pack of detergent, a few travel size packages of wet wipes (the greasy ones that are usually used for baby care are perfect and not desiccative) and of course shampoo and shower gel. A tote bag or a small gunnysack is perfect to store your dirty laundry. And can be used as a pillow. Earplugs can be a pilgrim's best friend. A torchlight is a better than a headlamp. You are a pilgrim, not a coal miner or Snow White's seventh dwarf. There is absolutely no logical reason to stumble with a headlight through the Spanish night. Not even a romantic one. Modern times mean modern items. Since almost everybody owns a Smartphone the damn thing needs to be charged. It's worse than those dumb Tamagochis from the nineties that wanted to be fed or amused every free minute. Buy a charging station. A cheap one for about 20 Dollars is sufficient as long as you can charge your phone twice without recharging the charger. Nobody steals a cheap charger. And if so, you don't mind.

What about the Walking Sticks?

In case you are used to a pair of walking poles, take them with you. Be sure you can rely on them. You need something solid you can rely on when walking downhill over pebble and debris. A reason why I prefer the singlehanded wooden stick is the solidity. The other reason is: I don't want to look like the guy who forgot his skis. And it gives me dignity. (This is not an attribute I am usually connected with).

About Training and some Health Advice

Well, to be true, there is no such thing as perfect preparation for something like the way. Of course it is helpful when your body is in a good shape, but to be really trained for a walk of more than two weeks you need to walk two weeks. Beside of your legs, bum and feet the muscles on your neck and back will have a lot of work to do. Your backbone and your spinal discs need the support of the muscles surrounding them. That's why I suggest doing endurance training AND some weight training, especially for back, chest and neck. If you are doing yoga: congratulations! There is nothing better to

22

get in shape and to gain flexibility.
When you walk, be sure your backpack fits
well, all belts and straps are fixed and the
pack is tight on your back and close to your
hips. If you make a rest somewhere, possibly
on the bank of a nice and cool creek or river,
try to resist cooling your feet in the water.
Your feet need to be absolutely dry before
you put on your socks again. Otherwise
blisters are a certain result! Blisters are
annoying but not a worst-case scenario. If
small, cover them with a plaster. If you use a
special blister patch, like "Compeed", do not
remove until it falls off by itself! Large
blisters can be punctured. Please be careful
and do not practice the trick with yarn or
twine pulled through the blister by a needle.
This is the fastest way to infiltrate the blister
with germs. Just puncture, let the fluid drip
off or squeeze it out, disinfect with iodine,
medical alcohol or disinfectant spray, put a
plaster or a tape on it and forget about it
until the next day. If you spoil your feet with
cooling and smoothing ointments every
evening and every morning before you put
on your socks, the risk of blisters is a
minimal one. A very good replacement for
an ointment that smoothes and refreshes
your feet is Vicks VapoRub.

What's Hot and What's Not: Some Pilgrims Etiquette

Helpfulness should be as natural on your way as consideration and amiability. Unfortunately thoughtfulness is an attribute that is not active in everyone's mind. Pilgrims do lots of things, even stupid ones, but a true pilgrim does not get up in the middle of the night making rummaging noises with plastic bags and turning on a lightshow with a headlamp. Some walk through the early morning hours in complete darkness and made their daily stage already at noon.

There is no need to hurry. There are enough beds on the way. No panic.

I already mentioned tote bags or gunny sacks. Please do not use plastic or paper bags for dirty laundry or such. Both make rustling noise when you pack your bag, and maybe other pilgrims around you are still asleep.

You are going to hear and say the salutation "Buen Camino" very often; pilgrims wish each other a good way, the people you are going to pass by will say it and sometimes you will hear a car honking. Spaniards believe it is good luck to greet pilgrims. So they do it from the cockpit of their cars too. A friendly smile is something everybody on the planet likes, even the grim looking elder gentlemen that are sitting outside the village bars. A friendly "Buenos Dias" or "Buenas Tardes, señores" will bring you good wishes for your own way. You never can have enough good karma.

In case you try to sleep outdoors, you better not do this in a field or a rural space. The Spanish farmers don't like it very much if their seed and crop is trampled down or if someone poops on their property. Most of them have mean, large junkyard dogs and shotguns. And please do not light up a campfire without permission.

Being the citizen of another nation does not allow you to violate or disobey the Spanish laws, nor does it protect you from punishment of local authorities.

Of course you can fill your water bottle at any well or fountain on the way. This is very romantic but very unhealthy. Even then when there is a sign that says "aqua potable" (drinking water). First of all, you never know which animal drank from the well and where it had its snout. (I don't know why, but most mammals are obsessed of sniffing other animals' private parts and residues). Secondly, most fountains are open air, and birds like to sit close to them on branches and birds do not care where they pee or poop. And thirdly, although the local people are used to their water, they prefer to buy their water in the supermarket for good reasons. The stomach of a stranger, not even used to foreign tap water, will not be pleased with the water of an open well. The water of a covered spring on a private property is something different. Don't worry about plastic bottles. Recycling is one of the strongest increasing industries in Spain. Ask in bars or shops where you can leave the empty bottles and show responsibility this way. It will be appreciated.

Other Pilgrims

"L`enfer – c´est les autres" "Hell- it's the other ones". The French philosopher Sartre used to say. Of course we do not expect hell on a pilgrim's path, but it is part of our humanness that we do not love each of our neighbours. The Camino attracts many people from many parts of the world and misunderstandings, displeasure, language borders and sometimes antipathy are inevitable. Here comes a short, and not to be taken too seriously guide to the most represented nations along the way:

The Spaniards: They are loud. They are proud. They are nice. In the blink of an eye you can get invited to share a bocadillo or a bottle of wine. Because the Compostela is a bonus in every résumé many young Spaniards walk the Camino or at least the last 100 kilometres. Since home growing is allowed they often smoke weed. In regards to the opposite sex, the men are shyer than the ladies. A well-educated Spaniard will recognize subtle signals from a lady, but never react on them until he is officially invited. Spaniards usually have a talent for other languages, but they try to avoid other tongues than their own.

The Germans: They are loud too, usually after the first bottle of wine. And they are smart. They even will correct a native speaker of a, for them, foreign language. Contrary to popular belief, they are humourous. Furthermore it can be said that Germans are very much interested in history, culture and other nationalities.
Their favourite leisure activity is to collect something. Like the Spaniards, the German men are shy. Germans appear sometimes a bit arrogant. They are only coy and not used to talking to strangers like Americans do, for example. Like the Dutch, most of the younger ones are able to speak one or two foreign languages. They do mistake a flirt often for friendliness, because they can't

believe it is really happening to them.

The Italians: Catholicism and lust for life means the same for them. They are devotional like a nun and lewd as a priest. All in all, the Italians like the company of others very much and feel lost when they are alone by themselves. To be surrounded by friends and family is for them "una bella compania". Food is for Italians even more important than sex. If you meet some friendly Italians at your albergue, you have a guarantee for a yummy dinner. Italians are not that much into foreign languages. Because of their ability to talk with gesture and expression, it is not difficult to understand them. They take every form of friendliness as a flirt. Un Italiano vero is incapable of imagining that a smile is just meant as one.

The Dutch: like their northern cousins, the Scandinavians, the Dutch are friendly, reluctant and well educated people. They often speak more than two foreign languages and it is not true that they all smoke weed. The truth is that only 30% of the Dutch population are potheads. Of all Europeans, they are in average the largest ones. Usually they are blond, good-looking and have real large teeth. It is said that they have a soft spot for Germans, which those never ever have recognized.

The French: the most chauvinistic nation of the entire universe, but charming. They can turn on the charm like others switch on a headlamp. While the females are usually open minded and curious, the French male is convinced of the cultural, intellectual, sexual and personal sovereignty of his nation. Usually they walk in small tribes along the way, on their search for seducible women. The French ladies usually have better things to do than to walk a few hundred miles over rocky roads; they prefer to take care of their appearances.
Languages: I already mentioned that the French are chauvinists? Even if they speak another language, it will not be before their non-French vis-à-vis has tried to speak a few French words, no way.

British: Of all British nations, the Irish are the best represented. They are friendly, hard-drinking and cosmopolitan people, which are always nice company. They like to sing and discuss and will lend a helping hand when needed. The often have cute freckles. Have I mentioned that they love to sing? On the Camino I have only met one person from England yet. She was a hard walking lady in her late 60s and had no problem to outdistance the younger pilgrims. On the British Islands foreign languages are quite unpopular.

Canadians: The most polite people on this planet. Very often they are educated and bilingual. They are sophisticated and true travellers. Canadians make a nice company and know more than 12 different ways to survive a blizzard.

Brazilians: The myth says that especially the ladies walk the Camino because they search for someone to marry. Well, I think there are worse reasons to walk the way. Brazilians are a friendly, nice and sometimes very sexy company, they are anything but prude and body talk is part of their culture. Many are able to shake their booty faster than a hummingbird can move its wings. This is called Samba.

South Koreans: Although Shamanism and Buddhism are the original religions of Korea, about 30 % of all South Koreans are Christians. But this is not the reason why the popularity of the Camino is increasing since a few years. About 30% is not religious at all. Like the movie "The Way" helped to make the Camino in the US very popular, in

South Korea a book by a local pilgrim had the same effect. The Koreans I met on the way were very nice and friendly people, who loved to experience anything new to them on their way. They have a talent for languages, and many love to take photos of their food. Pictures of octopuses from the restaurants of Melide are very, very popular. Those folks are called "Food-o-graphers".

US-Americans: Well organized and adventurous pilgrims. The Camino is often seen with misty–eyes by them. Some take the trip through Spain as the adventure of their lives, like the bull-run at the fiesta of San Fermin at Pamplona. Some take it as the cheapest holiday of their life, according to thirty-year-old copies of "Europe for Less Than 5 Dollars a Day". The American frankness and candidness is something that irritates Europeans quite often. It seems somehow lukewarm to us. When meeting someone yet unknown, Europeans try to keep a distance in the beginning. The mentality is completely different in many ways. Things which are talked about discreetly in Europe are treated publicly in the US and vice versa. Money, income and sex for example. For an American, it is quite normal to applaud someone else for his success and the status symbols he owns. In

Europe someone showing his riches is a parvenu, an upstart, an arriviste who will be more begrudged than applauded for his success. On the other hand, it is quite normal in Europe to talk about sexual topics in public. This is a thing that is not so common in the States and often misinterpreted as harassment. But with a little bit of open mindedness and common sense, all errors can be solved. For one thing I always envied Americans: they walk the way in amazement. Like no one else they are astonished all the time and open to the marvels around them. It is this open mind that makes them, most of the time, very nice and amiable company. Foreign languages are not their strongest point. While the average US gentleman after three days on the Camino has an appearance like a hillbilly in a slasher movie, the American lady hops maidenly along the way like Farrah Fawcett, Britney Spears and Jessica Simpson mixed together.

This is a good connection to another item of secondary importance:
Beauty culture and grooming.

How To Grow A Beard Without Looking Like A Wood Gnome & Other Unimportant Beauty Advices.

If you do regular foot care with callus removal, please consider that you need some hard skin on your way. So it makes sense to have the last foot care about 2 or 3 weeks before your way.

For many men, the Camino is the first chance to grow a beard. And after a few days they look as if someone has thrown a dead hedgehog on to their faces. Gentlemen, please do yourself a favour and carry a shaver with you, even if you want to grow a beard. Take a good look at old pirate and Zorro movies. The villains mostly had the coolest beards. Ask your local barber which style would suit you and try to cultivate it from the first day on. Most important tip: shave the neck in your throat area. A beard should end at the jawbone if you don't want to look like a badger or like Edward G. Robinson in "The Ten Commandments". In case you are used to shaving parts of your body regularly, keep that habit on your Camino or stop shaving a few weeks before you walk. Growing hair stubbles will make your way uncomfortable. For those used to depilation – don't worry, there are professional beauty parlors in every bigger city along your way.

Although weight is a very important factor on the way, I always carry my electric toothbrush and a scented after shave with me. There are minimum standards that a gentleman has to keep. Even if he looks like Wolverine.

Blisters, Bugs and Other Forms of Wildlife

The best way to handle a blister is to avoid it to begin with. If you keep the following facts in mind, the risk of blisters is minimized. (Ok, I repeat myself, but this is important) Foot care: start at home to get smooth feet – groom them with the ointment you are going to use on the Camino 2 weeks before you leave. On the way: put the ointment of your choice on your feet twice a day. And do not take a shower or wash your feet in the morning! Wet feet are moisturized feet and those get blisters. Quality socks, marked with L & R. Good, strong, reliable walking shoes, about two sizes larger than usual. Your walking shoes should be broken in. Walk a few miles in them before you set feet on the way. If you know you have a weak spot on your feet that easy gets blisters: put a good blister patch as prevention on the spot. There is one other suggestion (which I can't confirm, because I have never tried it myself): use a pair of thin seamless socks or nylons under the walking socks. Those have to be changed daily. The trick is that the friction happens between the two socks and not between walking sock and skin. But I do not know if this really works or if it is a myth. As I already mentioned: a hygienic and well-treated foot is one of the happy kind.

If you have blisters: if it is a small one and not directly underneath your foot (most blisters are on the toes and easy to cover) cover with a patch after your foot is dry and not greasy. The bigger ones: Just puncture carefully, let the fluid drip off or squeeze it out, do not remove skin, disinfect with iodine, medical alcohol or disinfection spray, put a plaster or a tape on it and forget about it until the next day. If unsure: ask at the albergues if they know a "blister doctor". You won't believe how many modern shamans and medicine men are on the way.

Bugs: well if you are born in New York, you should be used to them. For the rest of the world is the following information. Bed bugs are annoying but not life –threatening, if you are not allergic to them. The problem is, they are hard to kill, and the chemical instruments against them harm our health too. They often get carried from one place to another in a pilgrim's baggage. They love to hide in corners, gaps and cracks, in the dark, under or in a mattress. Wooden beds are paradise for a bug population. What can you do to avoid the problem? First of all, prefer albergues that offer bunk beds made of iron or synthetic material. No crack - no bug. The more popular the bed, the more bugs are living in it. You know how it is – obviously popular things are mostly the ones that are sold out first. Wallflowers are chosen last, but they are most of the time bug-free. The upper bed is the better choice. The more your body is covered by any kind of textile, the less the risk to get bitten by bed bugs. A silk inlet for your sleeping bag will not only keep you warm in the colder season and cool you in summer, but helps to keep the bugs away from your body.

Insecticides should be chosen carefully at home for impregnation of your textiles and your sleeping bag. Do not use them as a spray in dormitories! It is hard to say who is going to kick your butt first – the other pilgrims or the hospitaleiro. Remember: it happens more often that you are not harmed by bugs than bitten by them. Even when bugs might be living in the albergue you have chosen for the night. Some people never get bitten. So there is no reason to panic.

If you want to be sure if the mark on your body is really a bug bite and not a mosquito bite, just check if there are a few bites in a row. Bugs love straight lines and a geometric order. Treat the bites with a cortisone lotion – that's it. Try not to lay your backpack on a bunk bed. The less contact surface, the better. If you have a suspicion that your stuff might be infiltrated by bugs, bed-bugs die in the heat. So don't be afraid to put all your stuff in a washing machine or a tumble dryer. If both are not available put everything in a large black plastic bag, make a knot and let it heat up in the sun. One thing is for sure, high season is bug season. From spring until June, the risk is very low.

There is wildlife in Spain - with claws, beaks, teeth, spines, fangs, feathers, fur, exoskeletons and scaly skin. In other words: birds of prey, wolves, wolverines, foxes, badgers, bears, lizards, snakes, spiders, scorpions and other forms of life. (By the way: did you know that scorpions and spiders are close relatives to lobsters, crabs and crawfish? Astonishing – isn't it?). The chances to see one of the above-mentioned life forms are very low. What you are often going to see are storks, sheep, sheepdogs and maybe a fox. The sheepdogs herding the sheep in the mountains may be big and impressive, but they are friendly creatures. The myths and rumors about wild, ferocious dogs on the way are based on a mistaken passage of Paul Coelho. If you are the kind of person that is afraid of dogs: keep calm, ignore them, don't run and show self-confidence. It can be helpful to watch a few episodes of Cesar Millan´s Dog Whisperer in advance.

Discomfort and Dupery

Actually the way is safe. The next physician is never more than 15 kilometres away. The international emergency call number is 112. Thieves and pickpockets: The way is a reflection of life - there are heroes and villains. Keep your valuables close to you and please remember that it is the occasion that makes a thief. Frauds and con men are quite often to be found on the way. Those people know that a pilgrim is in very faithful mood, which makes it much easier to tell them heartbreaking stories which usually end with a request for money. Some try to disguise themselves as pilgrims, carrying shells and walking sticks. Most of those fake pilgrims are harmless and just beggars with a gipsy background trying to make some money. Remember: the international emergency call number is 112 and for any kind of emergency. **Advice**: take a second cell phone with you, preferably a cheap one, put a Spanish SIM card in it and you are prepared for emergency.

Take a Taxi

No, not for yourself. For your backpack! Sometimes it can be necessary or simply relieving to walk without your luggage. Some may call that cheating, but this is a very puritan point of view in my opinion. There will always be a stage that's really hard and sometimes you may not be in the best shape, so why not use a backpack-taxi? This service is called taxi de mochilla or trasporte de mochilla. The system is quite easy: At albergues, hotels and hostels you will find the information for the local mochilla trasporte. There are envelopes in which you put the amount of money the transport costs. On the envelope you write your name, phone number and your destination for the day (with the name of the albergue you plan to stay at). Attach the envelope to your backpack, leave it at the albergue's reception and have a nice day. Your baggage awaits you at your destination. Only two things have to be mentioned, because they are different to others: If you are going to Ponferrada, your backpack will mostly not be taken to the albergue. Instead they take it to a hostel called San Miguel. And in Monte do Gozo, they leave the backpack at the tienda de la calle, which you will pass by on your way to the Albergue of Monte do Gozo.

Links and websites

www.americanpilgrims.com: The US Pilgrims website.
http://www.csj.org.uk/: British fraternity of Saint James
http://www.santiago.ca/: The Canadian Pilgrims
http://www.csj.org.uk/australia.htm: Australian Pilgrims
http://www.stjamesirl.com/: Ireland

http://www.yourspainhostel.com: Excellent booking site for hotels and hostels.

http://www.alsa.es/en/: Spanish Bus tickets and schedules
http://www.renfe.com/EN/viajeros/: schedules and tickets for the train.
http://peregrinossantiago.es/eng/: The website to the pilgrim's office at Santiago, very useful!

https://www.caminodesantiago.me/luggage-storage-in-santiago-de-compostela/: is a link to a private luggage storage in case you want to send some of your luggage to Santiago. They store it as long as needed, while the Spanish post office stores only for 2 weeks.

http://jakobusfreunde-paderborn.eu :   a German website with excellent information if you are able to read German. If not, it can be helpful too: there is a link on the left side of the homepage which is named "Unterkunft" (Unterkunft = accommodation). This link contains a list of the stages. A click on each stage opens a list of all albergues on the stage. Although written in German the important facts are easy to understand.

So, that's enough good advice and wisenheimer stuff.
Let's move.

Leon. The Cathedral.

Walking diary
Leon, May, 11, 2012

The plane, taking me from Mallorca to
Asturias airport, is grounding on time. Since
I have my backpack with me as cabin-
baggage, I do not lose any time at the
luggage belt and make the bus to Oviedo last
minute. At the bus station of Oviedo I can
relax. The Supra bus with long-term
destination Madrid, that is going to take me
to Leon, will depart in one hour. For
someone not used to long distance travel
with busses, which are very popular in
Spain, the bus station appears a bit

confusing. Anyway, about 06.30 p.m. I have a comfortable seat under my derriere, a TV screen with cartoons in front of me and a glass of white wine in my hand while the scenery passes by the window. The mountain landscape, surrounding us, is of an untamed, harsh and rough beauty. Although it's May, there are still snowfields to be seen.

Right on time, at 08.00 p.m., the bus arrives at the beautiful old city of Leon.

I grab my backpack, take the phone and give my buddy Thomas a call. He is already since two days at Leon and recovers from the 570 kilometres he already had walked. He started his, meanwhile second, Camino at Saint Jean Pied de Port, on the French border of the Pyrenees.

Tom is forty, gay and a successful but unconventional businessman. He is as unpretentious as a cheeseburger, down-to-earth and a natural born renaissance man. With a scraggy beard and a wide grin in his face, he is sitting on the terrace of a bar in front of the gothic cathedral.

He hands me the key of his hotel room, where I can bail my backpack. The Hotel, named Paris, is situated round the corner and in the middle of the historic center. Five minutes later I have a glass of wine in front of me and Thomas reports all his mentionable adventures. He looks wild in a satyric way. Dark tanned, unshaved, with hair instead of hair-do and much more slender than three weeks before.

A young German peregrina joins us. Thomas knows her already. Her name is Melanie, she wears a Trilby hat, exudes a slight odor of weed and specifies herself as a lesbian. If she had hoped to provoke me with that opening, I have to disappoint her. Chacun a son gout. She turns out as a enjoyable drinking company and she's got a loud and hearty way of laughter.

We roam through the infamous "Barrio humedo", the liquid quarter, from bar to bar. Leon is beautiful, the wine is excellent, the tapas are rich and tasty. Along our way through the quarter we get in touch with many nice locals, have lots of chats and get invited to a few "chupitos". So it is no wonder that we get to bed a bit tipsy and very late. Well, that's what I call a prelude!

Some facts about Leon:

As already mentioned: Forget the albergue, take a hostel or a nice hotel. Leon is worth it! If you are on a bigger budget: Try the Parador Hotel, it is an ancient monastery and very beautiful.

Places of interest: the historic center of town, the barrio humedo with its Tapas Bars, the gothic Cathedral from the 13th century and the Romanic Basilica de San Isidro from the 10th century.
In opposite of the Cathedral the tourist and pilgrims information is situated. In case you are in need of it: Pilgrims credentials can be bought here too. A stamp worth to have can be received at the cathedral and the museum close to it.

The mountains of Leon

Walking diary
Leon - Villadangos del Paramo, May, 12, 2012

The night has been very short, so we have a breakfast for barflies: café cortado, a croissant and two aspirin to fill up our energy store. We follow the yellow arrows and the shell symbols that guide the way through the quiet town. As we pass the beautiful cathedral, we stop. I want to get my first "sello", the pilgrim's stamp, here at this ancient Gothic dome.
The dignified señora that stamps my credential, my pilgrim passport, looks a bit incredulous as I tell her that she has got the unique honour of inaugurating my credential. May well be she looks that way because of a small mistake I made in Spanish: instead of using the word "inaugurar" I used "desvirgar", which stands for "deflower". With a little sheepish wink and the brightest smile I can create, I try to dulcify her.
 The way, after we have left the historic centre, soon becomes a bit uniform. Housing areas, commercial areas, yet everywhere we pass, we hear a friendly, honest "Buen Camino!"
The Spaniards believe that it is good for their Karma to be friendly to pilgrims, which

explains too, why so many cars honk their horns, when passing us by.

It takes a while to get out of the suburbs of Leon. After eight kilometres, we have a break at a recommendable small bar named Virgen del Camino. Thomas is hungry and orders himself a Spanish tortilla, which is served here hot and fresh. I stay with a Kas Limon, a lemon soda pop I love to drink in Spain. I am not hungry at all. I only feel thirst.

The weather conditions are perfect. Sunshine, warmth, it's not too hot and there are no clouds to be seen.

A few minutes later we pass a church, all made of cement that may have been the latest in architecture in the early sixties. Very Bauhaus. Very ugly. Call me old fashioned, but the last time they built beautiful churches in this part of the universe was very long before industrialization.

So we follow the yellow arrows again, get a little bit off the original path, without really getting lost. As long as the sun is at our back we move in the right direction. At a farmyard, a peasant offers us water from his cistern, which is fresh and cool. We fill up our bottles and move further. Noon has passed and meanwhile I can feel my backpack. The muscles on my neck and back hurt. Seems as if I still have to learn how to fix and tie my backpack to my body. The road we follow is so straight, I have the feeling I can see the curvature of the earth. Thomas poses as my drill sergeant. "That's no curvature, you ignorant worm, that's our destination for today!" The infamous Khyber Pass! Full of heavy armed howling heathens! We almost made it! Do your duty! Chin up! Stiff upper lip! Aaaand march!" "Yes Ma´am!" I respond with obedience. About 04.00 p.m. we arrive at Villadangos del Paramo, which is a very long name for such a small town. My first stop. I am shattered. It would be easier to count the parts of my body that don't hurt, than those who do. But I am confident that this is just a temporary thing.

The municipal hospice, the albergue, is tidy and clean. We check in, move into our bunk beds, take the best shower since the invention of hot water, and groom a bit, then we head in Flip-Flops into town. It's Saturday and almost everything is closed for siesta.

The only two exceptions are a bar and a little drugstore, which they call here a "tienda". After we have taken aperitifs at the bar, we do some shopping at the tienda.

Two bottles of wine, some fresh bread, manchego cheese, air dried ham, olives and sundried tomatoes will be our frugal dinner. Back in the albergue, where we take seats in the garden, I discover Thomas has a very interesting talent. Although his foreign language knowledge is only rudimentary, he's got the ability to make friends among all nations. His voice sounds a bit like Ron Perlman as "Salvatore" in Umberto Eco's "The Name of the Rose", but he gets along very well. He already knows the two French middle aged couples from another stage of the way. They are sitting close to us, and he gets invited to a game of rummy. I take the chance to freshen up my French a bit and allow my back some rest, lying on a bench. After a short nap, I am finally hungry. So I unstop the wine and carve myself a sub sandwich, which a Spaniard would name a bocadillo. My bocadillo is as yummy as the wine. We are sitting together with the French, sharing and swapping our wines, olives and almonds. Strange, but after the small sandwich, I am satisfied. My sleeping bag calls me. Loudly. Tomorrow will be tougher than today. To our next destination Astorga, we must defeat 28 kilometres. And the terrain on the route will include a few adjustments in altitude.

Some facts about the stage Leon-Villadangos:

Length: 21 km, duration: 6 - 6.5 hours
Altitude difference: 90 meters
Breakpoints: Virgen del Camino; Valverde de la Virgen; The albergue of Villadangos is recommendable and situated at the towns entrance. Infrastructure in Villadangos: a supermarket, a bar, a restaurant, a tienda and a bakery.

Walking diary
Villadangos – Astorga, May, 13, 2012

Early in the morning at 05.30 a.m., I get introduced to a very special species of pilgrim.

The mining lamp - plastic bag – packer. With the bug torch around his forehead, he appears out of the dark like a Cyclops, rustling, coughing, sniffing and packing his stuff in as many rustling bags as he can find. Those will be stuffed with the largest effort of audibility into his backpack. Doing this he won't fail to be so diligent to shine with his mining lamp into as many sleepy faces as possible. Not later than six o'clock, preferably before sunrise, this early bird has flown. With a cheerful tune on his lips, presumably the "HiHo – Song" Snow white's dwarfs used to sing, he walks into the morning. A punitive look is not very helpful in a dark dormitory. So I try the dog education approach. A sharp hissed "Ksss!" works out fine with nasty dogs, anyway, the plastic bag packer shows resistance. I sigh, wish for a minute I was the dog whisperer Cesar Millan, and roll over in defiance to catch another 30 minutes of sleep.

In the following days I recognize that this sort of pilgrim is exactly the one who checks in already about noon in the next albergue on his route. The early rise is no evidence of health and fitness. It's a way of stockpiling. This pilgrim is a hamster, afraid he might not get a free bunk bed in the hospice of his choice.

At 08.00 a.m. we are on our way, my back is still stiff as a spade, but its getting already a bit better. At Hospital de Orbigo, we stride in adequate dignity over a medieval bridge. To be true, Thomas strides and I limp, but it is dignified.

Behind the pretty, medieval town, the way parts in two. We decide to take the longer, but more beautiful path. The uphill parts are exhausting. I am not in such a good shape as I thought I was. But the landscape is fair and beautiful, so I ignore the pain and follow Tom, who just started to intone different old fashioned German songs about the birds and the bees and the flowers and a romantic zephyr and lovely maidens dressed in nothing but moonlight.

Of course this is a very suitable behavior for a pilgrim.   On the top of a hill, in the shadow of an olive tree, we have a short rest. It is hot today, blue sky, not the smallest cloud in sight. In a small village, whose name I forgot, we meet Helmut The Frank for the first time, who sits in front of the only local bar with a glass of Rioja. He declares the thesis that red wine is a benefaction for human feet. He comes from lower Franconia, where theories like that are part of the local agenda.

At a high plateau, a few miles further, we come across some giant sheep dogs, even bigger than Tibetan mastiffs. These awesome dogs turn out to be cuddly, lovely creatures. A hundred meters later, we meet the flock of sheep and the shepherd, a likeable old man, and two more of those gentle giants, which look ingenuously at us while waiting to be stroked. Nine more kilometres to walk. We move on and suddenly, behind the top of a hill like a Fata Morgana, appears something that looks like an Indonesian food-cart.

The food-cart is close to an old barn, and in the shadow of a tree, a hammock and a kind

of Bedouin tent complete the exotic scene. I
expect the mad hatter or the white rabbit to
appear, but instead of getting offered tea out
of a bottomless pot, a guy named David
offers us fresh water and some Ayurvedic
juices. This eccentric oasis, called Casa de
los Dioses, belongs to two yoga addicted
drop-outs from Barcelona. Knowing about
my body's intolerance to vegan and
Ayurvedic food, and aware of the lack of a
bathroom for the next five miles, I stay with
water. We take a short rest before we walk
on. We pass the Cross of Santo Toribio and
have a great panoramic view from our
gazebo over the town of Astorga, which lies
down in the valley. A few hundred meters
before town we pass a strange iron bridge,
constructed like a horseshoe bend, painted
green as a frog and as ugly as a doodlebug.
One last ascent challenges us and then we
stand in front of the Albergue Siervas de
Maria, residing in an old convent. A roaring
"Hello darlings" cracks our contemplation.
It's Donna from Canada, who we have
already met twice on the way. She's about
60 with short grey hair, with shiny face
piercings and a figure like a heavy armed
dwarf from the Lord of the rings.
She beams at us with a broad smile every
time we see her. She always seems to laugh
and to carry a beer in her hand. She hugs us

passing by and lingers along in her flip flops. Donna is an incarnation for the lust for life.

Thomas feels an urgent need for a bathtub today, and resigns pilgrim romanticism in favor of a middle class hotel.

I check in at the Albergue, where I meet Helmut The Frank again, who is also an inhabitant of my little dormitory. I don't take the fact that the dormitory is in the second floor as an affront, but as a challenge. Damn. I can feel muscles I did not even know I had. This challenge is followed by a second one. The toilet seat is so close to the cabin's door, that a normal way of sitting down is not possible because of the narrowness and my muscle soreness. The only chance to get seated is to let oneself flop down. A solution that will not work for overweight persons! I reward myself with a hot shower.

One hour later we are sitting in front of a pizzeria at the Plaza Mayor, together with Gaby from Wisconsin, who invited us to join her. We order some local wine and enjoy the swarming on the plaza. Outside the hotel nearby, a Flamenco show is performed, and the dancers invite the tourists to join them. Well, everybody has the right to make as much fool of himself as he likes to. Our waiter shows us with ostentation that Astorga is more a touristy town than a pilgrims place. He ignores our trials to order some food. It takes some heavy Spanish cursing from me until he condescends to take our food order. Nonetheless the food is yummy. In my mind I send thanks to my Mallorquin friends who taught me such wonderful cuss words. The later it gets, the more locals appear. The whole town seems to be rambling along the Plaza Mayor. Kids are running around, playing soccer, teenager try to impress each other, pretty young girls show their beauty and as much skin as decency allows. They try to catch the young men's' melting gazes and look disinterested at the same time. Elder gentlemen sit together in severity, playing cards and chatting. Elegant señoras walk arm in arm with amenity and dignity under the colonnades. I always admired the chic and style of the ladies from the south. Even as elders, they punctuate their femininity in a distinguished way.

Compared to that, we Germans and Celts are such bumpkins!

Some facts about the stage Villadangos-Astorga:

Length: 28 km, Duration: 7-8 hours
Altitude difference: 100 meters
Breakpoints: San Martin; Hospital de Orbigo; Santibanez de Valdeiglesias; San Justo de la Vega
The albergue Karl Leisner at Hospital de Orbigo is famous and has a good reputation. The Albergue Siervas de Maria at Astorga is very recommendable and offers lots of facilities. Places of interest: The ancient Bridge of Hospital de Orbigo and the town itself; The Oasis "Casa de los Dioses", run by the gentle Yogi David – perfect for a rest! The Cross of Saint Toribio: a perfect view into the valley of Astorga and to the Mountains de Leon in a distance. The Cathedral Santa Maria, the Bishops Palace constructed by Antonio Gaudi and the Town hall on the Placa Mayor. Astorga is a town for those addicted to sweets: there is a chocolate museum and a manufactory for excellent cookies and chocolate. The evenings on the Placa Mayor are perfect for every dallier: life is like a show on a catwalk there.

*The bridge to Hospital de Orbigo
and the way to Astorga*

The way to Manjarin, above the clouds

Walking diary
Astorga - Foncebadon May, 14, 2012

After breakfast in a nice little bar, we leave
Astorga. We are facing a tough stage today
and decide to try a little experiment. The
"trasporte de mochilla" is a service offered
at almost any hotel and hostel. A taxi will
bring our backpacks to our destination,
Foncebadon. We put some Euros in a
prepared envelope, add the address of our
destination, tie it to our backpack and leave
those at the reception of the albergue. That's
it!
Close to the old palace, constructed by
Antonio Gaudi, I buy myself a beautiful
wooden walking stick. During the following
days I will get very used to it, like Professor
Higgins to Eliza. The stick is quite helpful
and grants some safety walking downhill on
debris. It grants too an air of dignity and
gives me a sort of prophet's attitude. Every
once in a while, I have to overcome the
temptation to bless by passers.
The weather is gorgeous. After a few miles
we leave the country lane, and pass through
blooming heathlands. In a distance appear
two peregrinas with heavy luggage. It takes
just a few minutes to reach them. They don't
hesitate to ask us where we have left our
baggage. Thomas smiles in a very pixyish

way: "Backpacks? We don't have any. We trust in God. The way will supply us with anything we need," he says in a very preachy tone. "Amen brother," I add. "By the way, do you ladies have some spare toilet paper and some small change?" As wild as we two are looking, with bandanas, tattooed and unshaven, the two ladies believe us for a New York minute. But Thomas is still a bit puckish. Next he asserts that his name is Joshua and he's an acolyte of the famous prophet Saint Ibu, the inventor of the even more famous painkiller Ibuprofena. His job would be to distribute the pills like altar bread to needy limping pilgrims. He waves with a package of pills and says,"Say aaahh!"

We are in a walking mood. So we leave the two ladies behind and pass a beautiful village, lying completely deserted in the sun, like the residence of a bygone vampire clan. Every cottage is built of natural stone, some bumblebees dawdle through the air and a mistrustful cat lingers on a corner. It's getting hot today, we fill up our store of drinks at a soft drink machine, which appears a bit absurd in this rural setting. After a few kilometres we arrive at the hamlet of El Ganso, where we decide to take a rest. The only bar around is called "The Cowboy Bar" and is as sleazy as a saloon in

60

a Sergio Corbucci movie. We resign to visit the toilet at this place as well as to order some water. Instead we take two alcohol free beers, which we drink after having cleaned the bottleneck with a germicide cloth. Later, back home, we discover that this bar is as famous as it is notorious. Every pilgrim seems to know it, and it seems to appear in almost every movie about the way.

On the way to our next subgoal, Rabanal, two women from Austria overtake us. The two walk as fast as mountain goats, and because of male vanity, we share their speed for half an hour before we reduce to our personal speed limit. In between they suspect us to be some kind of fun-pilgrims and Tom is even suspicious to be a kind of spring-breaker. We decide to have some fun, and disclaim their suspicions by explaining that we've been working in pastoral professions. We look after loose women, orphans and would be the honorary spiritual guides for the Hells Angels chapter at Munich. These arguments incite some jaw-dropping. "No! Really?" " No, just kidding. Actually we are retired founding members of the Chippendales. Now a days we do some pole dancing and stuff like that for charity reasons. Do you fancy a lap dance?" I catch a penal gaze from the lady on the left of me and a hysterical giggle from the other one, before they begin to accelerate. "Hey… wait," I shout after them. "It's for charity!" Tom and I are grinning while we watch the two ladies disappear.

A bit later we arrive at Rabanal, where we rest for a longer time. We are facing a difference in altitude of 400 meters and a distance of 6 kilometres to Foncebadon. At Rabanal we meet Helmut The Frank again, who joins us on our way to the formerly abandoned and now revitalized village of Foncebadon. Thomas is considering spending the night outdoors at the Cruz de Ferro, the famous landmark, thirty minutes behind Foncebadon. The Way leads us constantly uphill and I am very glad that I don't have to carry my backpack today. I sense every muscle and can even feel my gluteus maximus growing. My perception of the day: long distance walking is good for a firm butt.

The mountain landscape around us is wonderful. Far below us Astorga can be seen, and close to the horizon we can guess the shape of Leon. The Way is rocky and rough, lizards scurry over the stones and every now and then we see birds of prey high above us. We are passing a flock of sheep, and their massive canine protectors watch us in typical Mastiff fashion: laid-back and even-tempered.

Finally we arrive at Foncebadon. And our backpacks await us already. This experiment was successful. My neck is still tensed up and I am very glad to find out that they offer massages at the Albergue Monte Irago. Helmut and Tom decide to spend the night outdoors at the chapel in front of the Cruz de Ferro, and fill up their stocks with two bottles of red wine and some bread and cheese. Outside the albergue, in the rays of the afternoon sun, we share a few glasses of Rioja and arrange to meet the next morning at the iron cross.

The hostel is very hippystyle, Buddha statues and Hindu gods make a big part of the decoration. I get a bed in the Yoga room and take a long shower. Then I come to appreciate the benefit of a massage by Martina from Sweden that soothes my skin and melts my muscles. I catch myself in the mirror, a light sunburn on my shoulders, my face and arms took a shade of bronze. A nice contrast to my grey beard. Well, even a pilgrim has a right for a little vanity.

Later, sharing some wine and food, I meet a nice old Spanish gentleman. Conferino is already 80 years old and walks el Camino for the second time. He's a sporty and tough guy with more hairs on his head as usually destined in his age. The stories he's telling are very amusing although I only understand half of it, it doesn't matter. We get on together fine. He reminds me a bit of my grandpa, who I am still missing, 32 years after his passing. He has same slender and strong appearance, with hands large as a frying pan that testify to a laborious life.

Some facts about the stage Astorga - Foncebadon:

Length: 26 km, Duration: 6-7 hours
Altitude difference: 600 meters
Breakpoints: Murias de Rechevaldo; Santa Catalina de Somoza; El Ganso: Good place for photos and a beer, no need to rest here for the night; Rabanal del Camino: The albergues of Rabanal have a good reputation. For Those who think of walking to Foncebadon in the morning a good place to stay.; Foncebadon: 3 Albergues. Recommendable by the authors' experience: The Albergue Monte Irago.
Behind Astorga are just a few shops and many bars but no ATM until Ponferrada!
Places of interest: The landscape; the completely weird Cowboy bar at El Ganso; Foncebadon itself.

Thomas & Helmut after a night outdoors

Walking diary
Foncebadon - Ponferrada May, 15, 2012

Every day has a new insight. This morning I
learn about a local pilgrim-species that I dub
the double P: Parrot-Pilgrims. This variety is
one that takes getting used to. It is a
combination of early bird and chatterbox. A
very loud one. It seems everybody in the
dormitory knows each other. As soon as
their blue Spanish eyes are opened, their
mouths and tongues start working. I have the
theory that these organs are somehow
connected in a strange evolutionary way.
They giggle and cackle and snicker and

babble and narrate without drawing a breath. Now I know why I dreamed just now about strolling in an Asian fish market.

Less than one hour later, after a cup of strong coffee and some bananas, I am on my way. At 08:20 a.m., I face the famous Cruz de Ferro that looms on a hill of debris and stone. The sky is as blue as silky French knickers. I can feel the significance of this place, where for thousands of years, pilgrims carry stones from home and then lay down this material representation of their burdens. When so many souls pray and meditate at one place over such a long period, they leave traces that can be felt by every halfway sensitive being. With a paint stick I drew an OM symbol, my name, and today's date on a little Flintstone that I found on a shore in Denmark 15 years ago. I place it on a stone column not to drop a burden, but I believe it is good Karma to follow ancient traditions. Looking to the right of me I discover Thomas and Helmut The Frank. They are already awake, sitting under the porch roof of the chapel. They still are in their sleeping bags, grinning and looking scrubby. "So guys, how was your night? Any wolfs, wild dogs or dingos?"

"Naw… everything fine and quiet. With the exception of the screams of the foxes round here." Thomas smiles. "If there would have

been some predator, I would have fed them with The Helmut." Helmut keeps the countenance and dignity, that suit his age and gives Thomas nose a light nudge accompanied by a friendly "beep!"
While the two are getting their stuff together, I have a phone call with my mum, who celebrates her birthday today and presumably is worried about her son. She is glad to hear from me and yes….she is worried. In her imagination, I am on a walk through the absolute wilderness, far away from any civilization. Dr. Knud Livingston on his expedition through the black heart of Spain. "Mom, you've been watching too often Apocalypse now! There is no Colonel Kurtz around here. I swear!" I send her a photo message to assure her of my physical integrity.
Helmut decides to take it easy today and Tom and I walk on. Far below us we can see the clouds, above us only blue sky. We are on the highest point of our walk. The summit we passed is over 1500 meters high. At the abandoned hamlet Manjarin, we stop for little while at the hermitage of Tomás, the self-proclaimed Last of the order of the Templar. There he stands, in his robe, a large ankh on his chest, his arms based on a sword and holding his morning speech to a bunch of pilgrims. I do not understand very

much, but I understand that he gives the bypassing pilgrims his best wishes and blessings. The scene touches me much deeper than any church service can. Somehow Tomás reminds me of the humble Buddhist monks I met in Thailand. And Tomás is doing good deeds without pretence. Every year he rescues Pilgrims that have lost their way in the mountains. Here and now, in bright sunshine, it's hard to imagine, but in rain and snow it's very easy to get lost on the way in the mountains. He is some kind of dropout that got stuck on the Camino. Maybe Tomás is a weirdo, as nuts as the mad hatter, the white rabbit and the dormouse all together, but one of the good kind. The salt of the earth, the knee of the bee.

The Way is going downhill and the decline is steep. Now I am very glad to have my wooden Pilgrim's stick.

For some unexplained reason, the song "The Weight" by The Band pops up in my brain and so I am walking and humming until we reach El Acebo. We have a rest in that pretty village; the local tienda offers anything a pilgrim might need. I am in need of an isotonic drink. An alcohol free beer and two hardboiled eggs make a nice picnic. Thomas got a tortilla, which makes him happy. A guy from Netherlands and an

Italian beauty, that we ran into a few times recently, are waving at us. The connection between the pilgrims is great. Somehow everyone knows each other from bypassing, from the albergue, from a short chat or another situation. And of course everyone wishes the other a "Buen Camino!"

Leaving El Acebo we pass a memorial, forged out of the remains of a smashed bicycle. It is dedicated to a German bike pilgrim who died here, accelerating in the curve. We follow the yellow arrows and leave the road. The Way is getting rocky, full of stones and debris. We cross small creeks, walk through cool oak woods, by bushes of broom and wild olibanum. Sometimes we have a little break, smoke a cigarette and enjoy the sun, the silence and the sound of early summer surrounding us.

After a few hours we arrive at Molinaseca. We enter the small town over an ancient bridge, overstretching an untamed little river. The bridge leads us directly to a bar at the bank of the river. We take off our shoes, let our socks gasp for some air and are taken by surprise that the flies around us are not falling stone-dead from the sky. We ask for two beers and two dishes of croquettas. Thomas doesn't know this yummy food yet. In Germany they are hard to get. In Spain they are an essential part of the cuisine.

These potato croquettes are made of a filling of minced meat, fish or ham mixed with a béchamel roux and deep fried. Very delicate and satiable. Tom thinks about spending the night here at Molinaseca. It seems as if the night outdoors was not as refreshing as he asserted. Helmut The Frank arrives too. He wants to go to Ponferrada today. So do I. While my companions are still resting I hit the road for the last eight kilometres of the day. This stage is boring and takes me over country roads without any shadow. It is hot today. I pass two more monuments raised to remember pilgrims that have died on the way. It's good to know that the names of those who remain here will not be forgotten. At the entrance to Ponferrada an old man offers me something to drink. Although I still have enough in my water bottle, I accept thankfully. The only albergue in town, San Nicolas de flue, is a very large one, very Catholic and the folks who are running the place seem to be a bit bewildered. My phone rings. It's Thomas who has checked in at a small hotel close to the Ponferrada castle. Helmut has arrived at the albergue meanwhile too. While he is standing in the kitchen, cooking a buckhorn plantain extraction for his feet, his circuit collapses. Five minutes later he is awake again, asking himself why there are so many worried faces around him and why he is laying on the floor. "This fanning of fresh air with your fan is very refreshing, young lady, and my current position is very comfortable and attractive, but thank you, I am fine by now" he addresses to a sorrowful looking girl that has been bedding his head in her lap. "Isn't he a charming little devil?" I say to ease the situation. From the outside we can hear the sound of the siren as the ambulancia rushes in. They give him a check up as intense as a drug squad officer would check the Grateful Dead's tour bus. In contrast to Jerry Garcia's hiding places, they don't find anything. Helmut shrugs, gives the still worried looking girl a graceful smile and decides to take a little nap.

I walk into town then and meet Thomas below the magnificent Templar castle. We walk through the historic centre to the Plaza Mayor, where we have a few beers. During dinner, Thomas is very silent. He is a bit exhausted and tired. So he heads for his bed soon. I stroll to the albergue, where I sit in the garden, together with some other pilgrims from all over the planet. A surf style guy from Canada shares a small doobie with me; the moon is reflecting the light of the sun and some bats are flying around in fractal patterns. The background noise of talk, laughter and the clangor of beer bottles and wine glasses soothes me like a Spanish nurse's lullaby. As I arrive at my four-person chamber, I climb to the upper floor of my bunk bed and fall asleep easily.

In the middle of the night, I learn about three new pilgrim species. The weak bladder, the bunk bed vibrator and the lady that confuses me with her hubby. First the weak bladder wakes me up. Incapable of leaving for the bathroom in a silent way, she makes more noise on her bare feet than a marine in high heels on an iron fire ladder. The Italian, from the lower bunk bed under me, is next. Obviously he has problems falling asleep without touching himself. Through my own experience, I know that it is even possible to get laid in absolute silence. Without vibration. But it seems that the prejudice is right. Italians don't do anything in a silent way. I bang my fist in a very considerate way against the bed frame and try the "ksst!" It works! As soon as I am asleep again, someone shakes my bed. It is the lady from the upper bed next to me. No, she is not in a flirty mood. What a pity. Well, may be I snored a bit. "Marry me and you can shake me as much as you like to" I murmur and turn around.

Some facts about the stage Foncebadon - Ponferrada:

Length: 28 km, Duration: 7-8 hours
Altitude difference: 100 meters uphill; 1000 meters down.
Breakpoints: Cruz de Ferro; Manjarin: The weirdest Albergue on the entire Camino is Tomas place. The last Templar knight has atmosphere to offer, but no water from the tap or reliable electricity. A stay here is a special kind of adventure; El Acebo: 2 Albergues; Riego de Ambros: a municipal Albergue; Molinaseca: good alternative to those who don't want to spend the night at Ponferrada, 2 Albergues; Ponferrada: just 1 large Albergue and many small hostels and hotels.
Infrastructure: bars and Restaurants all along the stage; at El Acebo a tienda, at Molinaseca shops and pharmacy; At Ponferrada anything a larger town has to offer. Some ATM´s.
Places of interest: The landscape is great: the descent starts at 1550 meters above sea level. If you are lucky you might see the clouds below. Places of interest: The hermitage of Tomas at Manjarin. Don't miss his speech! The memorial for the bike pilgrim forged from the remains of his bicycle, at El Acebo; The ancient bridge that

*leads into Molinaseca and the lovely river it
crosses; The Templar knight castle at
Ponferrada from the 13th century and the
baroque town hall of Ponferrada from the
17th century.*

Helmut The Frank

Walking diary
**Ponferrada – Villafranca del Bierzo May,
16, 2012**

Obviously my three bedfellows were early
birds, and I was so tired I did not notice their
departure. At eight o'clock, Thomas and I
share a pilgrim's breakfast at the bar of his

hotel, consisting of café con leche, an energy drink, croissant and cigarettes.

Along the Templar's castle and through parts of the historic centre we walk, looking for the yellow arrows to guide us. As we leave the historic part of town the surroundings get boring. The avenida we walk on is as exciting as the centre of an Amish town and as charming as a motorway service area. At the rusty looking blood donation monument we turn to the right, pass some bigger road constructions, which remind us that life goes on in spite of pilgrimage, and walk finally on rural roads again. We enjoy the company of Finn from England and Adriana from Germany. Finn is actually no pilgrim. He's a backpacker, walking along the way for a few days without credential and insignia of a pilgrim. Adriana calls herself a light pilgrim. It's her first day on the walk. Our stage today is not very straining, we decide to take our time and walk with an easy beat. Already in Fuentes Nuevas, we enjoy an extended break. Thomas decides to have a silly day. For no other reason than the boredom of sobriety, he is already beer thirsty and has his first two beers of the day before the clock strikes ten. That is a bit too early for me, so I remain with alcohol free beer.

Shortly before Camponayara, on the bank of a fast flowing ditch, Adriana and Finn take a longer rest while we walk on and come to pass vineyards. In almost every village we notice stork's nests. The weather is wonderful and we simply have a nice day. At the town of Cacabelos, we made more than the half of our day's stage. It is a pretty little town with a nice and cozy plaza, where we come to rest. We order some food and Thomas continues to cure his sobriety with beer. Half an hour later, Helmut The Frank shares with us his pleasant company, followed by a nice elderly couple from Saxony. For reasons no one could ever explain, the blond dyed hausfrau has the odd idea that Thomas would make a fantastic son-in-law.

Helmut and I have had enough rest and are impatient to move on, like greyhounds at the races. Thomas in contrast feels more like a sloth and decides to stay a bit longer and practice some German "Gemutlichkeit" in the company of a few beers. So he will meet us later in the albergue. As we walk away from the plaza we wave at him and sing Jackson Brown's "Oh won't you stayayay … just a little bit longer..." It takes some time to leave this town. The road that leads out of it is sparsely populated, but it's still Cacabelos. We pass a funny looking albergue. Around a church, small two-bed cabanas are arranged, which look like the Italian Seaside dressing rooms from resorts in the early sixties. Very charming. I make a notice in my mind to stay there for my next Camino. It's hot today, there is almost no shadow, and we are grateful for every small tree. Finally we leave the asphalt road and enter a field path, where bushes and small trees are growing. We are both relieved. Shortly before our destination, Villafranca, my phone rings. It is Thomas. The voice that comes out of the phone receiver is full of despair, like a tortured soul from the depth of the purgatory. "Knud, please….help me... I don't know where I am… I am laying in a meadow at the side of the road…I'm devitalized, there are already vultures floating over me….I am dehydrated." I need to laugh. "Dear Thomas, as long as you can pronounce words like dehydrated, everything is fine and the vultures are storks. So, come on and hit the road. We are waiting for you at the albergue Ave Fenix." Helmut giggles as I tell him what Tom said. Generally Helmut is a pleasant company and he knows a lot about wild growing herbs and medical plants, which is a very useful skill on the Way.

A bit later we enter Villafranca Del Bierzo. We come to pass the municipal albergue on the right, where a few peregrinas are fixing their unmentionables to a clothesline. Close to the church from the 12th century is the famous albergue Ave Fenix. The atmosphere is gorgeous. Behind ancient walls lies a kind of caravanserai for travelers, backpackers, pilgrims and dropouts. This iconic place is run by a guy named Jésus Arias. In the little shop an excellent choice of local wines is offered as well as postcards with the image of Jésus. Water, coffee and tea are offered for free. I like this place immediately. A blond flower child in harem pants, called Vera, does the check in and offers the possibility for pilgrim's dinner, which we appreciate.

Tom arrives a bit later, grinning and halfway sober, but still thirsty as an archbishop. Finn and Adriana are making a short stop. They met two Spaniards who are going to give them a lift to the village of Vega. Adriana gives me her phone number, just in case. Well, that was a short acquaintance. While Thomas is taking care of his thirst and Helmut his hygiene, I take care of my laundry. The washing machines are marvelously old fashioned, but they do their job. Forty five minutes and two glasses of wine later my laundry is done. I fight my way through masses of T-shirts, socks, towels and a large collection of lingerie hanging on the clothes lines until I find enough space for my stuff. I get myself a fresh beer and lean back in anticipation of dinner. The dinner is simple but good. I notice my appetite just in the same moment as I have the first spoon of vegetable soup. Later we all are sitting together in the yard, share our wines and stories and meet some new folks we haven't met before.

There is the eighty year old rambler with this big bushy beard who looks like the blacksmith from Tombstone city. The weird Frenchman they call the Ukulele, the tough Bavarian couple, the strong rouged middle aged lady, who seems to take the Camino as some kind of lonely hearts speed dating. She is doing her best to sit and move in ways that shall demonstrate the willingness to flirt. Anyway – it does not seem to work. Then there is the little Dutch peregrina that can't roll cigarettes, Alberto from Brazil, who is here for a few weeks as a hospitaleiro, and Vera from Russia, who has lived in Spain for twelve years and is addicted to the Camino. In the thick of it, Thomas and me. In case of present early birds and mining lamp owners we decide to inform everybody, as a preventive measure. "Ladies and gentlemen, may we please have your attention for a minute! We just wanted to inform you that everybody who's making

noise or a mine lamp light show before six
o'clock in the morning, is going to be
punished. Very hard. Thank you!"
Tomorrow it's going to be O´Cebreiro.
Camino duro - the hard way.

Some facts about the stage Ponferrada – Villafranca:

Length: 25 km, Duration: 6-7 hours
Altitude difference: 100 meters
Breakpoints: Fuentes Nuevas: good place
for a short break, no Albergue;
Camponayara: a normal Spanish town, no
real Albergue, just an emergency
accommodation; Cacabelos: very popular
Albergue build in a 1920´s seaside resort
style and situated around a church, the first
(mentionable) Pulpo and seafood
restaurants on the way; Villafranca del
Bierzo: 3 Albergues, the most famous but
notorious is The albergue Ave Fenix. It is
very Hippy style, more tweedy than neat, not
the perfect place for someone sensitive or
persnickety. I like it!
ATM´s at Camponayara and Cacabelos,
many bars and shops on the way.
Places of interest: a nice and tacky chapel at
Cacabelos, the Pulpo restaurants of
Cacabelos; The 12th century church Iglesia

*de Santiago at Villafranca. Here they gave
to pilgrims, who were to sick or old to cross
the next mountain, the emergency
Compostela. That's why Villafranca used to
be called "Little Santiago".
The wines of the region El Bierzo are rich
and tasty!*

Walking diary
**Villafranca del Bierzo – O´Cebreiro May,
17, 2012**

Very unexpectedly, we are quite early on
our way. Two bananas and a coffee make

some kind of breakfast. Until we reach Trabadelo we walk along the national route N VI and we are pretty fast. My body is now accustomed to the demands of a long hike; only the right flatfoot tries to argue sometimes with me. But what the hell, he's just a foot and only a sixth of all my extremities. So I silence my foot with some Ibuprofenas, which he seems to like. I am afraid my right foot is a pill addict.

Tom and I concentrate just on our steps; we both have a kind of tunnel vision this morning. The beauty of the landscape, the surroundings and the villages we walk through somehow fade into a blur. Until Ruitelan, we move on fast, and now the road is uphill again. We take short, steady steps. It is not possible to walk as if in the lowlands. On long uphill distances my pulse is very speedy, so I feel for it sometimes on my neck. Thomas is amused and declares the gesture with two fingers touching the cervical artery to a new form of pilgrim's salutation.

Every time I have to rest to catch some breath, I say things like: "Oh look, how beautiful this (add some wildlife of your choice) is!" "Oh yes, very beautiful," Thomas usually replies. "It is astonishing how green this nature can be, isn't it?" When he is out of breath he pretends he has to pee. Not even an incontinent Chihuahua can piddle so often!

Shortly after noon we arrive at La Faba. In the moment when we are taking off our backpacks for a longer rest, a scratchy horn honks close to us. Vera and Alberto from the albergue Ave Fenix are grinning like Cheshire cats from the interior of their old multicolored Renault. They are taking an 80-year-old guy from Canada up to O´Cebreiro. Impulsively we hop into the car. Its 4 kilometres until O´Cebreiro, those last 4 kilometres are steep and hard and would take us about two hours. "This is not very pilgrim like!" I wag my head in a critical way, like a first lady discussing morals. "May well be," Tom answers, "but we save about two hours, have a nice rest in Cebreiro and walk on to Triacastela. Whattayathink Doc?" He gives me a look like a very fluffy version of Bugs Bunny. I take a look into my pilgrims guide and I am pleased to find out that the ascensions after O´Cebreiro are halfway harmless. "Okay, let's do it! If we are done with that, we have a double stage today of a bit more than fifty kilometres. That's an acceptable penance for hitchhiking, better than praying a rosary anyway."

A few minutes later we are at O´Cebreiro. The famous village is a hot spot for tourists and bus tours. A large bus ejects a whole bunch of them, swarming like flies through the souvenir shops with their daypacks, high heel sandals and make up conserved by air-conditioning. This village, giving shelter to pilgrims since the early 9th century, has become a Disneyland version of itself. The church is worth a visit and the straw covered roofs remind me very much of a smurf village. I grew up, for a part of my childhood, in a Saint Mary's place of pilgrimage and the apathetic and disinterested faces of the merchants here remind me very much of the rosary dealers I used to know. The place is pretty, and still looks very original, but the whole impression leaves a bad taste in my mouth. We take a rest; Vera and Alberto join us. We share stories and adventures. Vera is from Russia and has lived in Barcelona for over twelve years. From time to time, she heads out to the Camino and to the world's end, Finisterre. Usually she takes her time, with longer breaks in places she likes and she works for food and bed in albergues. She has an independent lifestyle, free of bondage and necessities but, also free of safety and guarantees. Alberto the Brazilian is a funny guy. Humorous, always a broad smile in his face and often a glass of wine in his hand, he spreads sympathy like a lifeguard on a tropical beach. He too took much time for his Camino and stayed in different albergues as a helping hand. Now his time in Spain is going to end. In a few days he will take an airplane home to Rio de Janeiro. It's strange, but short talks with those who were once strangers strengthen the feeling of affiliation to the pilgrim tribe. We bid each other farewell, pack our bags and start to walk on again. Including breaks, we hope to reach Triacastela at the later afternoon.

The old chestnut tree of Ramil

***Some facts about the stage Villafranca –
O´Cebreiro:***

*Length: 28 km, Duration: 7-9 hours
Altitude difference: 830 meters uphill
Breakpoints: Pereje; Trabadelo; La Portela
de Valcarce; Ambasmestas; Vega del
Valcarce; Ruitelan; Las Herrerias; La
Faba; La Laguna; O´Cebreiro; Albergues at
each mentioned village. The Albergue of
O´Cebreiro is very popular and has about
100 beds to offer.
Infrastructure: lots of bars and tiendas
along the way. The last ATM before
Triacastela is to be found at Vega.
Places of interest: The landscape is
incredible! The Camino Duro - the hard way
– is a beautiful way too. O´Cebreiro is a
smurf village and popular among coach trip
parties. At O´Cebreiro the yellow arrows
have been invented by a local priest in 1984.
Now you have entered Galicia!*

The church of Villafranca do Bierzo

Walking diary
O´Cebreiro – Triacastela,   May, 17, 2012

As we leave O´Cebreiro, our tunnel vision
leaves us too. Even when the Way gets
steep, we are in a good mood. We sing silly
songs, then stop sometimes for a moment,
just to enjoy the beauty of the landscape. We
walk through wonderful, blooming
heathlands and as we look back, we can see
the mountains we crossed. After one hour, a
lovely old British lady with white hair is
overtaking us. She is wearing two Nordic
walking poles and walks in a rhythm as

steady as a Singer sewing machine. No matter if uphill or downhill, she keeps the same speed and rhythm. "I bet at home, she's the leader of the pack in the city park", Thomas says, as she disappears behind the next curve. Well, the senior citizens these days aren't the same as in our youth. We decide to become rebellious, stubborn and adventurous retirees, as soon as we retire. As we ascend the Alto do Poio, which is the last summit we have to reach, we meet a Spanish farmer, old as the hills. We exchange greetings and a few words. He seems to be the senior peasant of the farm we just passed, and is walking a few times daily up to the top of the Alto do Poio just to have a few glasses of wine. We are fairly impressed. He sends us with a friendly, toothless smile and a "Bon Camino" on our way. At the top I am exhausted for a few minutes. Near the path we are walking on runs the road on which the old British lady appears. She took the road instead of the path we walked on, so we could overtake her in spite of her steady walk. Behind her arrives a weird apparition. A pilgrim without a backpack but with a carriage he bonded to his hips. It seems he carries everything with him that a traveler would need for a trip around the world. We can identify a tent, a mattress and a large solar cell-powered charger. I can bet there must be a TV and a pizza baking oven in the depths of the cart. There are not so many pilgrims on the road at the moment. The reason must be the quite late hour. Most of the pilgrim's bunches are likely one or two hours ahead of us.

After a short rest we walk on. The old British lady has already left 10 minutes ago. About half an hour later we meet her again. She is sitting on a stone wall, coughing like a non-smoker in a Cuban cigar manufactory. We join her and try to take a bit care of her. "Seems as if I caught a bit of a cold, no reason to worry," she says. "The next albergue on the way will be mine." I take a look in my guide. The next albergue is in Fonfria and just 2 or 3 kilometres away. We decide to accompany her. Thomas takes her backpack, against her protestation, and straps it to his chest. Half an hour later we arrive at the small village of Fonfria. The British Lady is called Karen and is coming from Cornwall; she is a widow, 68 years young and walks the Camino for the second time.

In the albergues garden we sit down on wooden benches. Karen insists on inviting us for a few beers. I check my pharmaceutical stock and find a small bottle with "Klosterfrau melissengeist", a Melissa Spirit (which is such an old form of German self medication, that its roots are lost in the mists of time) that is very helpful for colds. Karen tries them and is pleased to state that this medicine tastes like Jägermeister. After she checked in a single room at the albergue, we bid farewell. Thomas is a bit worried if she is really okay. I calm him down.

"What's up? Have you got your grandson - ish day?" I tease him. "You know what its like. Everybody does his own way and Karen is old enough to know what's good for her."

As we pass the entrance to Triacastela, we have a wonderful walk behind us through sunny woods and green meadows. At a little bar we drop our backpacks and rest for the while it takes to sip a glass of white wine, before we follow the signs that guide us through town to the different albergues offered here. The municipal albergue is already booked out, the first private one we see, behind a supermarket, is a bit shabby and the two women responsible for it leave a very sleazy impression. The next on our way looks neat but is booked out. At the Albergue Aitzena we find our beds for the night. The owner is a nice and charming señora in her best part of the fifties; the rooms are spacious and the common room is homelike. As we handle the formalities we hear a voice calling for Thomas. "Hey

Tom!" A young man sitting at the old oak wood table between other pilgrims waves at us. He looks at me. "You got to be Knud. Right?" I am a bit perplexed, but have to laugh. "Seems as if Thomas is trying to make me a legend. I wonder to how many pilgrims he announced my arrival." The young guy laughs from the heart. "To almost everybody between Pamplona and Leon, as far as I can tell." His name is Mustafa and he is coming from Stuttgart. He is one of the young Turks from the third generation, born and raised in Germany. With him are two ageless good looking ladies from Sweden and an older athletic Italian named Claudio. We excuse ourselves and vanish to take care of our beds and a hot shower. We share the room with a Spanish couple, on their way as bicycle pilgrims. They talk a very broad Catalan language, which reminds me immediately of the mountain villages of Mallorca.

After a simple but tasty dinner of bread, cheese, meatballs in tomato sauce and some wine, we stroll through the alleyways which are home for the most bars and restaurants in town. We meet Melanie, from our Fiesta night in Leon, again and a redhead named Doris, which Thomas knew from Burgos. The night is warm, but around the moon clouds do appear. Maybe it will rain soon.

After a bottle of local red wine and two glasses of Cuarenta y Tres, we go to bed. "Good night, John Boy!" Thomas says. "Good night, Mary –Ellen," I respond.

Some facts about the stage O´Cebreiro – Triacastela:

Length: 22 km, Duration: 6 hours
Altitude difference: 280 meters
Breakpoints: Hospital da Condesa: small Xunta Albergue; Alto do Poio: Albergue and Restaurant. Not a very remarkable place, but good for a refreshing break; Fonfria: very rural place with excellent Albergue in beautiful surrounding. Nice garden.
Restaurant and bar; Biduedo; Triacastela: 5 (or more) Albergue. Recommended by the author: Albergue Aitzena.
Infrastructure: Bars, tiendas on the way, at Triacastela supermarkets, bars, pubs, restaurants. The ATM is only available when the bank is opened.
Places of interest: The Col of San Roque with an often photographed pilgrim's monument; the landscape and hundreds of Spanish cows which are mooing around and an 800 year old chestnut tree at the village of Ramil.

Walking diary
Triacastela - Barbadelo,   May, 18, 2012

It is, according to the fact that Thomas, me
and the Spanish couple have the same
groovy rhythm while we snore, a remarkably
silent night. We may be making sound, but
we don't hear it. For me it is as silent as the
night before Christmas. I wake up as fresh as
a rinsed crystal glass, there is summer in the
air, the birds sing and barefooted maidens
dance around the oak
trees…ooops…daydreaming again. It's
raining. My Macintosh has its first job to do.
We head to a little cafe where we have a
freshly brewed café con leche. Tom shrugs.
"That's the way I know Galicia – wet." The
rain is a gentle kind of drizzle; we are
thankful it doesn't pour. We walk along
small roads and forest tracks that lead us
through a landscape that seems almost Irish
or Breton. Well, the Galician descends from
the Celts. The word stem of Galicia is
"Gaelic" and the knotted patterns, found on
crucifixes and monuments along our way,
and last not least Galicia's situation on the
stormy coast of the Atlantic prove the
cousinship to the Celts. And – the Galician
folks do love the ear-polluting
sound of the bagpipe. The woods we are

walking through do seem absolutely magic. I
would not be astonished if some
Leprechauns, fairies, dwarfs or little red
riding hood herself would bang around.
As we take a short rest behind San Xil, we
see in the distance a larger group of pilgrims
moving towards us. The closer they get, the
more they seem like the magnificent seven
on their way to next showdown. And one of
them wears a Stetson. I am tempted to roll
an imaginary Sombrero in my hands and say
something like: "Perdon Señores, Banditos
have-a robb-ed me village" Tom smiles.
"It's Ben Cartwright and his sons." He is
almost right. They are not the Cartwrights
from the Ponderosa Ranch, but the Müllers
from Neuschwanstein. At the age of 76,
Daddy Müller took backpack, stick and his
porkpie hat, told his four sons something
about those boots that were made for
walking, and got on the way. His sons are
between 30 and 45. Altogether they make a
cool bunch. Daddy Müller is one of those
elder gentlemen that cannot deny that they
were some kind of lady-killers in their
younger days.
Depending on who is having a rest we
overtake each other quite often today. As we
pass a one-horse town, an old Spanish
countrywoman offers us fresh and hot
tortilla, which is more than yummy. With a

94

"Buen Camino" she waves us good bye. A few kilometres later we meet Katja. She seems to be a bit bored with walking all alone, so she joins us. She is in her twenties and appears to be one of those well-bred, docile girls. We find out that she knows a lot of really dirty jokes and bad words in sign language. Ok, not docile. And she knows a lot of songs that would fit very well at a Boy Scout convention mixed with songs from the repertoire of the Salvation Army. She sings soulfully, but with a gleam in her eyes that shines like the sins of the angels. Because of the fact that a choir is more fun, we change to German pop songs from the 60s and 70s. To illustrate how terrible (but well known: we had only 3 TV Channels until 1985) these songs are, please imagine some really bad shmaltz sung by people that look like a mongrel between Bobby Vinton, Sonny Bono and Alice from The Brady Bunch. As we finish this repertoire we switch to British glam rock. So the Galician woods are enchanted by the immortal sounds of T-Rex, The Sweet, Smokie, Suzy Quatro and the world infamous Showwaddywaddy. Afterwards Thomas tells the famous Bavarian legend of Alois the baggage porter. Which goes like this:
Alois the porter lived in Munich and died one day all of sudden. As he arrived at the

pearly gates, he found out very soon that there was no beer available in heaven. And as he was told there was nothing else to do but play the harp, rejoice, jubilate and eat manna, he was so disgusted and angry that the "Hallelujah" he sang sounded like a growling bear. All the angels complained about his behavior. Even the archangels said he was a pain in the ...bottom. So the Lord decided to send him back to Munich, as his personal ambassador to the Bavarian government. As soon as he was back in Munich, he went straight to the famous Hofbräuhaus. His favorite waitress, the beautiful and charming Anneliese, served him a beer. She served another one and a third, and as he meditated a little bit about the aesthetics of her bosom, he forgot about his duty. And because of the fact that he is some kind of immortal, he is still sitting there.

Katja giggles, "What a strange story." Thomas replies, "The more Catholic the country, the more hearty and colorful the legends." In the early afternoon we arrive at Sarria. The last 100 kilometres until Santiago begin here. At the Rua Maior we take a seat outside of a tapas bar; the pilgrims menu is good and cheap and we are very hungry. A few steps away from us, I notice two strange looking individuals. Dark

skin, like the people from the south of India,
thick, shiny greased hair, faces like
Lebanese second-hand-car-dealers. They
carry each a pilgrim's stick with a
symbolized calabash and a St. James shell
knotted to it, but they don't wear walking
shoes or any other kind of hiking equipment.
Obviously some gypsies, trying to make a
fast deal in disguise of a pilgrim. Thomas
notices them too. "The closer you get to
Santiago, the more frauds you will see. The
thing is that trustful and helpful pilgrims are
much easier victims to frauds than others.
The pilgrim heart is so filled with joy, that
he has difficulties to see the evident. At
Leon for example is a scrounger around that
tells pilgrims the heart-melting story of a
lost train ticket and her sick mum. She got
even me. And I am a cynic. " We nod and
shrug. Well. That's life. The predators have
become smaller and more harmless since the
Middle Ages but the prey is still naïve and
credulous.
Half an hour later we are on the way again.
We take a few steep hills in the woods as we
overtake a group of American teenagers
hiking around in deck shoes and sneakers.
They have only just begun their walk in
Sarria. From now on we will see much more
short distance and weekend pilgrims. The
albergue where we will stay tonight is called

Casa Barbadelo and seems to be quite new. It's a beautiful place, the larger bunk bedrooms are already booked out, but there is still a four-bed room with private bath available. We are excited. It is great to have the chance to groom oneself in a private environment! And the best of it is that the beds are not bunk beds, they have fresh bedclothes and tonight our sleeping bags stay in their cover. The albergue has a little tienda and a souvenir store. So we buy some food, some wine and have a seat on our little front porch. The door to the room close to us opens and someone we know is stepping on the porch. It's the two Austrian women, that walk as fast as mountain goats and which Tom and me spoofed a bit. Although they suspected us to be some kind of spring-break pilgrims, they are quite nice. Tom still appears a bit dubious to them. This is why he can't stop to wind them up. This time he swears he'd be the principal of a finishing school for young, well-educated ladies. Of course they don't believe him. "Ok, now please the truth! What's your profession?"
 Thomas sighs. "Ok, the truth is…. We both are screenplay writers.
Most of the time we do feminist pornography. He writes the plot and story and I write the dialogues. It's not as easy as it sounds. All that squeak and groan and

moan must be handled with care." Katja and I can't help it. We laugh so hard that we got stitches. "Sorry Ladies, but meanwhile it's a running gag." We cheer with our last sip of wine. The sun sets and we leave our shoes outside the door. I do the smell test. And I take a big breath through my nostrils. Nothing. No smell, no fug, zero, nothing, nada. I must say, there is nothing much better for a pilgrim than those high-tech socks.

Some facts about the stage Triacastela – Barbadelo:

Length: 23 km, Duration: 6,5 hours Altitude difference:
300 meters ascend 400 meters descend Breakpoints:San Xil; Montan; Calvor: one Albergue but no bar or restaurant; San Mamade: Albergue with dinner and breakfast; Sarria: many Albergues; Barbadelo:3 Albergues. My favorite is the Albergue Casa Barbadelo with bar, restaurant, shop, laundry service. Infrastructure: Until Sarria only a few possibilities for a break. Sarria offers shops, supermarkets, ATM´s, restaurants, bars and a pilgrims and outdoor shop.

*Places of interest: the so called Horreos,
small buildings erected on stilts are a
common view in this part of Spain.
They are used as granaries. Sarria exists
since the times of the Roman Empire and
has been re – founded in the 12th century.
Many buildings from the 18th century in the
part of town that the Camino leads through.
The monastery Santa Maria Magdalena
exists since the 13th century.*

Walking diary
Barbadelo – Gonzar ,   May, 19, 2012

Katja is an early bird. About six in the
morning she is already in her boots. Half
asleep I wave good bye and turn around. The
early bird might catch the worm, but I prefer
some bakery products. At seven Thomas
yawns. "Oh…Katja is already gone?
Haven't noticed her departure at all." "Yep,
about six this morning, I guess you chased
her off by your snoring." "Me??? I don't
snore!" I get the giggles. "Thomas, you
snore like a flock of dying walruses!"
After a light breakfast we depart. The
landscape is dominated by woods, forests,
small romantic villages and fields. All in all
it's very green. We could be in Ireland.

The whole territory is wild and untamed, the natural green here would overcharge any painters color palette. It looks like a film location for the Lord of the Rings. A sign in the woods informs us about the native animals and plants. We learn that these woods are still a home for bears, wolverines, polecats, vultures, eagles and many other predators as well as for a bird called the wood grouse. During our walk we sometimes feel a little bit playful. So we greet strangers and pilgrims we meet with a friendly "Pax vobiscum" or "Dominus vobiscum, giving them some blessings as we walk by. Thomas calls it a walk-by-blessing, the pious version of a drive-by-shooting. We don't even shrink back when singing a soulful "Ave Maria". Although we do not know the lyrics as well as we should. In church service, during my childhood, I sat most of the time on the last bench, playing blackjack. But I still get the priestly intonation quite well.   Tom has nothing better to do, than to shoot the nonsense we do with his cell phone cam. "Ever since he's got his pilgrim stick, he became this way. I can't help it, not my fault. I expect him to walk on the next stretch of water we pass by!" I have to grin and Thomas' words remind me of the Rolling Stones song

"Faraway eyes", which is a wonderful stultification of each bigot redneck.

It starts to drizzle and as we arrive at Portomarin, dark clouds are hanging from the skies in a very fateful and theatrical way. I am in need of an ATM and Thomas was struck by a sudden craving for pizza. So we drag ourselves up the tantalizing stairs that mark the entrance to Portomarin. At the arcaded sidewalks we walk to the next best pizzeria. As soon as we have the first sip of wine, rain comes down like a cascade. For a short moment it seems to take a break and then the rain accelerates. This is a flash flood, a universal flood, a Noachian deluge. "Let's take a boat", Thomas murmurs between two bites of tuna pizza with anchovy and artichoke. "Look! It's over!"
The rain vanishes to do his job somewhere else and some sunbeams linger, still a bit shy, around the corner. We know our priorities and so we visit first the church from the 12th century and afterwards the local supermarket, where I get seduced by a bunch of gummy bears. From behind a shelf jumps Donna from Canada in our way. "Helloooo Daaaarlings!" It's great to see her, she is such a likable person and absolutely unique. We have a few beers together and leave a bit later for the last seven kilometres.

The albergue Casa Garcia at the village of Gonzar has a good reputation. In the late afternoon we arrive there. Three charming young Spanish ladies take care of everything in the albergue. Before I get the chance to take a shower, a bottle of cool white wine is on the table and my dirty laundry is in a washing machine. These girls are charming and efficient! Around the large oak wooden table pilgrims from all over the planet are already assembled. There are Dutch, Irish, English, Americans, Italians, German, Austrian, French, two Koreans and some Spaniards (which still have a siesta in their bunk beds). Three of the pilgrims I met already on the way. There's Katharina from Germany and James and his girlfriend Carol from Eire.

After I had the chance to refresh, I walk towards the lovely patio and one of the American guys asks me: "So what do you think? Who will win tonight?" Bayern München or Chelsea?" Oh, damn. It's the finale of the Champions League. Usually I don't care much about soccer. To be honest – even the hidden secrets of the breeding of blue haired lowland sheep are more fascinating to me. But – hey, I am living in Munich, so in the middle of Galicia I have to show some local patriotism. The girl that checked me in catches this ball. "Oh yessa,

whatta you thinke? Who will win?" I smile
at her and take the chance to shine with
some of my indecent Spanish. "Guapa, no
tengo ni puta idea."
Guapa, dear reader, means "pretty woman"
and for the rest – well, feel free to get a
translation by yourself.
While Tom and I are sitting at the bar with a
good bottle of local red wine, a guy called
Clyde from Montana and three girls from the
mountain region of Austria join us. Clyde
spends his life travelling because of the
enviable fact that he is an heir by profession.
We share our wines and stories; all in all the
chats and encounters are a bit lukewarm, but
likable. Sometimes skin deep is deep
enough.
Thomas and I agree to split up for a while.
 Walking alone belongs too to the Camino,
being alone with your thoughts, to focus on
ones self, to meditate while walking. Not
later than at Santiago we will meet again. In
the last few days we became closer. Okay,
we were friends before, but here, on the
Camino, we deepened our friendship and
knowledge about each other. In daily life,
one meets his friends from time to time,
mostly in comfortable situations like a party,
sports, barbecue or whatever. The intensity
of the friendships we used to have as kids
gets lost the older we get. It's Life itself that

makes it harder: the bonds and duties of job, family mortgage and loan. And while we are sitting there, facing the second bottle of red wine, I understand that the Camino already gave some real good things to me. I am, in spite of some little aches and pains, as relaxed as a stoned Deadhead. The last time I felt so laid-back, I was having a few beers with some Surfers at sunset on a Balinese beach. I decide to take much more care of my friendships from now on, to listen more intensely to my inner self, to be more attentive to others. A book of Jiddhu Krishnamurti, one of 20th century greatest philosophers, I once read, comes to my mind: "The Flames of Attention". Somehow I feel a bit like after a long meditation, but may be it's only the wine. We salute each other. A glass of red cures any kind of sentimentality in an instant.

Some facts about the stage Barbadelo – Gonzar:

Length: 26 km, Duration: 7 hours
Altitude difference:
400 meters ascend and 400 meters descend
Breakpoints: Peruscallo; Morgade: small
private Albergue; Ferreiros: Xunta
Albergue; Villacha; Portomarin: 8 or

105

meanwhile more Albergue; Gonzar: 2
Albergue. Very recommendable and one of
the best on my 2012 way is the Casa Carcia.
Great place, nice bar, good service!
Infrastructure: drinks and food along the
way. In Portomarin: Shops, Supermarkets,
ATM's, bars, restaurants etc.
Places of interest: Behind the hamlet "A
Brea" is the 100km marker stone to be
found. The barrier lake of Portomarin and
the bridge that crosses it. The original town
in sunken since the 60's in the floods. The
church of san Nicholas, from the 12th
century, has been deconstructed in the old
sunken town and reconstructed in the new
town. This is the region for a brandy called
Orujo, which tastes a bit like grappa and is
available as "Hierbas" in a version with
herbs too. Excellent after dinner.

Walking diary
Gonzar – Palas de Rei,   May, 20, 2012

Today's stage won't be that long, so I can
afford the luxury of sleeping until 7:30 a.m.
I have planned the stages of my
glorious arrival at Santiago on the 23rd of
May carefully. Most of the stages are quite
short. Theoretically I could arrive at

106

Santiago late in the afternoon of the 22nd, but I am not in such a hurry.
I enjoy a strong coffee, grab my backpack and short past 8:00, I am on my way. Half an hour later I have another short coffee break at a small bar along the way. Outside the bar, sculptures of Don Quixote and Sancho Pansa greet the clients. Both do not seem to belong to the Camino but somehow, in a weird way, they make sense. Thomas is already ahead of me, as far as I know, he wants to make some miles today. It is different to walk alone. I do not meet many pilgrims, my thoughts meander around a bit and I allow my brain to run free, without any selected target. Out of the blue appears the idea to write this
book. Different wordings and phrases find their way from the bottom of my imagination into my mind. A frame starts to take some shape, not ready but recognizable. Like a stickman it is walking through my mind.
A bit later my mind asks for some quality time and decides to surf around a bit. It is great not to be focused on a specific thought. The sky is cloudy and blue, turning into a very French kind of bleu at the horizon. On the edge of a forest, I take a rest on a stump. I am all alone and I start to meditate. My eyes fix upon an old mighty oak while my

mind tries to stop thinking. This is harder than it sounds. I help myself with a classical meditation technique. I follow the way of my breath through my body. I imagine how the air flows from my nose through my chest, my spine, until the flow reaches the tips of my fingers and toes. After a short while I am sunken in perfect relaxation. Because of the fact that almost everything I do is somehow connected with a memory, it is not very astonishing that I remember, while meditating, how my Dad taught me to meditate. The conscious way of breathing, how to sit like a Buddha, the position of hands and fingers and the concentrated view on a distant point until the eyes snap on to infinity. Half an hour later my mind is empty and my heart is filled.

I am aware that many, who walk the way, walk it with lots of questions and expectations. Those questions and expectations about God, epiphany and enlightenment? I don't have them. I know who I am and what the universe expects from me. I am who I am. The way I am is good for me. The experiences I made on the way until now just fortified this opinion. Another benefit I made is the experience to enjoy the simple things much more. It can be so relieving to be reduced to a minimum of comfort, to carry all your belongings around in a backpack.

I arrive about 2:00 p.m. at Palas de Rei. At the Albergue „Buen Camino" I find a place for the night. In the Albergues backyard, I see Donna enjoying a beer and the sun. Beer. What a lovely word. Sounds good to me, and so we are soon sitting together in the sun. With a beer. Donna tells me that she lost her way a little bit today. "But I never felt lost" she says. "I always know where I am. I am always HERE. The problem sometimes is that I am not always sure where this HERE might be!" I have to laugh. I just two sentences Donna explained a lifestyle in a funny way and has been philosophical too. I ask her to tell me a bit about her life. A lady in her sixties with an overwhelming lust for life which shines out of every cell of her body (with a large collection of piercings) is anything but trivial. So she tells me that she grew up, until she was 12, in Canada amongst Inuit, far away from any kind of civilization. As far as I understand, her father used to be some kind of explorer and scientist. She still speaks the Inuit language. Her husband is a pilot and she has grandchildren. We talk a bit about the special relationship between grandparents and grandchildren. I tell her a

bit about my life and we exchange e-mail
addresses.

I feel my empty stomach. Since I have
been walking the Camino, I do not eat that
much during the daytime, just light and
healthy stuff. I get hungry in the afternoon.
In a little restaurant I order a pilgrims menu
for nine Euros. I have pasta,
chicken, an almond tart and a glass of wine.
Through the windows I can see Katharina
walking by. I wave her in; she is
accompanied by Eva from Brazil Food tastes
much better with nice company. And of
course we share stories. "Have you seen this
guy? And what has happened to that lady?
Did you know that…?" Well, even the
Camino has its gossip.

Eva feels a bit overfed after dinner, so we
order some Hierbas, an herbal brandy,
served in frozen glasses. After dinner, both
are a bit tired and move to their bunk
beds. Opposite of the restaurant is a small
pub, where I take a seat next to James and
Carol who just arrived. I discover that
James and I both like the 80´s band The
Smiths very much and so we have a large
topic to talk about. The glass of wine, they
serve here, has the absolute unbeatable price
of 80 Euro Cents. The mix at this place of
locals and pilgrims is very funny and
pleasant. I try to learn a few words

of Gallego, which I forget before I stroll over to my albergue.

Some facts about the stage Gonzar – Palas de Rei:

Length: 18 km, Duration: 5.5 hours
Altitude difference:
200 meters ascend and 150 meters descend
Breakpoints: Hospital da Cruz: good for a short coffee break; Ligonde: small Christian Albergue with dinner & breakfast; Areixe: Xunta Albergue; Poros: small private Albergue; Palas de Rei: 4 Albergues and hundreds of beds with facilities like laundry, Wi-Fi etc.
Infrastructure: bars and restaurants along the stage.
At Palas de Rei shops, bars, restaurants, ATM´s and even a not expensive pilgrims store.
Places of interest: Behind Ligonde is a beautiful Gaelic cross to be seen. Instead of the crucified Jesus the theme is a Pieta of Mother Mary holding her dead son. The Pieta is surrounded by the typical Gaelic knot patterns.
The tree close to the cross is said to be very old too.

Somewhere behind Palas de Rei

Near San Xulian

Walking diary
Palas de Rei - Arzua, May, 21, 2012

In the words of John, Paul, George
and Ringo: It's been a Hard Day's Night.
Although I am dead-tired, I am already on
the road at 7:00 a.m. The Spanish folks I
shared my dormitory with were really sweet
and lovely people, but one of the elder ladies
had some bad and very loud respiratory
problems. She was gasping and rattling and
snoring like a drowning bull moose.
Sometimes it sounded like a hibernating
bear, sometimes like a burning steamboat
and sometimes like a critical incident at the
zoo. The young Spanish guy from the
lower part of the bunk-bed looked at me
from sleepy eyes and nods in the direction of
the bed that produced such primeval noises:
"Bien dormido? Mira! El oso Gallego
en su habitat natural!"   The Galician bear in
its natural environment. I have to laugh so
hard, I am still giggling as I leave
the albergue.
At 7:30 I pass the small village
San Xulian and its
neat albergue "O Abrigodoiro", where I
decide to have a café cortado.
Inside, Claudio, the Italian guy who I met
in Triacastela, is sitting surrounded by three
pretty young Korean girls. He grins like

a first-time-father short after birth. As I look around I notice how beautiful this building is, all made of natural stone. Next time I will skip Palas de Rei and stop here, I promise myself. And meanwhile I am sure I will walk the Camino for a second time. Four days ago I was not so sure about that. Claudio and the three degrees want to walk to Arzua today, like me. So we walk together until we reach Melidé, a town famous for its octopus dish. We stop for a meal of boiled Galician kraken at the famous Pulperia Ezequiel. A delicate meal of pulpo with bread and white wine for just eight Euros.
Back home
they normally serve those chewy, deep fried pieces of calamari that taste as if they've been taken from the grumpy cartoon character, Squidward from Sponge Bob. But this taste is fantastic. The pulpo is as soft as butter, tender and with
an intense flavor. It is boiled in
saltwater, and afterwards swung in olive oil and spiced with paprika. Before cooking, the pulpo gets a special treatment. Like I know it from Greece, the pulpo gets hit and whacked until the strong protein structure is loosened. In my mind, the Ramones sing "beat on the brat…with a baseball bat... oh yeah…"

Ji Sun Tracy, Hannah and Jihae Kim are the
names of the three ladies who enjoy
the pulpo as much as I do. Hannah, the
youngest one, lives in Seoul and is a student,
Tracy lives in Hong Kong and Jihae in
Singapore. Jihae and Tracy have
known each other since childhood and are,
though just about 25, already successful in
working life. Tracy belongs to the thirty
percent Catholic population in Korea, and
prays before she starts to eat. That touches
me somehow, because the silent way she
prays is so unsophisticated and
genuine. Jihae is a tomboy, always in
motion, only silent when chewing; she
laughs and giggles most of the time. With
some people this can be enervating, but
with Jihae, it's part of her personal charm.
Hannah is a silent girl and sometimes she
leaves the impression of being a little bit
sad.

 After lunch we set off. The girls and
Claudio walk a fast beat. They almost march
as snappy as a bunch of WestPoint cadets at
the President's visit. I prefer a beat more
andante, so I let them march along. By the
end of the day I will meet them
in Arzua again. I enjoy the day, meet some
pilgrims from other stages again, we sit and
share the usual "who's where and what and
why" and then separate again.

116

A few miles before Arzua, I catch up with Claudio and his adoptees. We walk into the not very remarkable town together. At the albergue "Ultreia" we find a nice accommodation. As soon as we relax with a glass of wine, Mustafa arrives too, followed by a nice guy from Denmark called Ib. So we are a large flock of pilgrims that steps into the next best restaurant for dinner. The pilgrims' menu is simple, good and satiable. Claudio, Mustafa and I buy a few rounds of Hierbas that help to digest. So it is not so surprising that Mustafa comes up with a brilliant and ambitious idea. "What do you think, my dear fellow pilgrims, if we take a double stage tomorrow? At one go, directly to Monte do Gozo. The next morning we could walk with the sunrise the last five kilometres to Santiago." I check my guide. The distance from Arzua until Monte do Gozo is about 35 kilometres, there is almost no mentionable inclination and I like the idea. Everybody at our table does. We confirm the decision by oath and buy a last round of Hierbas. At the Albergue, two bottles of Rioja and some good tempered pilgrims from Uruguay await us. Two of the Uruguay women whisper as they look at me. Then they giggle and grin. "Hombre, you really look like Mickey Rourke!" Tracy noticed that. "Who is Mickey Rourke?" The two Uruguayans start to list Mickey's most important movies. "9 ½ weeks, Angel heart, Rumble Fish, American Graffiti, Barfly, Year of the Dragon…" But Tracy does not know even one of the mentioned movies. Too young. I haven't heard the comparison with Mickey Rourke since the early 90´s. Until now, I thought the resemblance had washed out through the years. Well, obviously not. In spite of my Pop Hemingway beard.

Some facts about the stage Palas de Rei - Arzua:

Length: 29 km, Duration: 8 hours
Altitude difference: some easy ascends and descends
Breakpoints: San Xulian: Very recommendable Albergue; Campanilla: the Bar Los dos Alemannes is nice for a short rest; Casanova: Xunta Albergue; Lebreiro: small emergency Albergue; Melidé: 2 larger Albergues and the best Pulpo along the way – perfect for an excellent lunch. Very famous and well known is the Pulperia Ezequiel; Castaneda: small private Albergue; Ribadiso da Baixo: Neat and historic Albergue – very popular; Arzuá: 6 or more

Albergues: recommendable by own experience is the Albergue Ultreia, comfortable, neat, nice bar. Infrastructure: Bars and restaurants along the way, ATM and bank at Melidé and Arzuá. At both cities many shops, supermarkets and restaurants. Places of interest: The Pulperia Ezequiel at Melidé and the cheese shops and bars at Arzuá where they make a cheese called "tetilla" ("Titty Cheese") because of its breast like shape. It is said the middle age farmers designed the cheese that way as a form of protest against downsizing the breasts of female statues in the cathedral of Santiago. (Which really happened. In the early middle age the stonemasons had a more fleshly imagination about the looks of female saints and Mother Mary.) But may be it is only a special kind of cheese-maker humor. Who knows?

Making new friends

Walking diary
Arzua – Monte do Gozo,   May, 22, 2012

Today's stage is a challenge, so from yesterday's dinner, I am the one who hits the road first. I am sure Mustafa, Claudio and the ladies are going to overtake me in the next few hours. After a two-hour walk, I receive a text-message from Thomas; he seems to be somewhere in the woods 20 kilometres away from Santiago and he is tired. He has met two hard drinking ladies from Austria last night, who outplayed him easily.

Meanwhile, I think it is time for a break and "Hey, presto!", after the next bend a bar appears. The bar seems to be very popular among pilgrims. It is very well visited. The walls are covered with graffiti, tags, sketches, haikus and poems (or what the authors thought a poem might be). Many of them sing the landlords praise. A German girl with an eye-patch asks me about a large monument, a statue of Jesus that should be around here somewhere. She is looking in every other direction but mine, though she is asking me a question. I believe that this is a bit impolite and pretend to think about that. "Well, the only large statue of our Redeemer, shall his name be praised eternally, that I know is to be found in Rio de Janeiro. That's a little bit more westward as far as I know. But I might be wrong. "I give her an encouraging smile, but she rolls her eye and makes clear that she takes me for meshugge. I don't mind. Being a little bit bonkers never hurt anyone.

As I walk on, I get into a regular trot, which takes me to thick eucalyptus forests. The air smells like koala bear farts and cough lollies. Before I realize what has happened, I have walked three hours nonstop. Now there are no more real highlights along the way, pure nature dominates. For a few minutes I follow two young Spanish guys that try to

121

impress a young American lady who walks with them. She's a pretty blonde, with a sportive shape and a worth-to-look-at butt, swinging like jelly in her tight shorts. One can tell that she knows about the impression she leaves. Of the two guys, one is speaking, and the other one translates. I can catch a large part of the monologue. The speaker seems to be a holier-than-thou young man; he maligns the behavior of other pilgrims nonstop as bad or inadequate. It is significant that he does not even drop a short "Buen Camino" as I overtake them. Well, seems as if I met on my next to last day the sanctimonious kind of pilgrim too.

Half an hour later, as I get hungry, I reach a hamlet. In front of the only restaurant, Thomas is sitting, looking crapulent. Close to him is a small dog that enjoys the leftovers of Thomas' Tortilla. I order a large portion of Croquettas de Jamon and ask Tom to tell me of his latest adventure. Until yesterday he made good progress, walking mile by mile, until he met those two ladies from Austria, who must have been really bad barflies. He shakes his head: "Never. Again. Alcohol. No more. In. My. Entire. Life." I am quite sure that he will have forgotten this oath as soon as we are at Santiago.

For the first time, since we walk together, it is now me who dictates the rhythm. Like Baron Samedi on Mardi Gras leads the second line dance, I lead Thomas who follows me stumbling. He scuffles behind me and every five minutes he grumbles: "Don't walk so fast…." I feel like Maya the honeybee, being followed by her friend Willy, shouting: "Maya! Don't fly so fast!" Approximately 8 kilometres until we reach Monte do Gozo. I decide to cheer up Tom's mind a bit and compose to the melody of a popular nursery rhyme a song about Saint Ibu the prophet. Fifteen minutes later we both do sing full-throated. Fancy a sample? "I smell like a polecat and a skunk, feeling like a saint and looking like a punk… they call me Ibu, the pill addicted saint, savior of the wimp and protector of the faint…." May be not the best piece of lyrics, but we had fun with it. At a raunchy bar, close to the airport area of Santiago, Tom is disturbed by something in his shoe. "This can't be true!" He shouts. "780 kilometres without any problem and here, just a stones throw away from our destination, I get myself a blister. And the damned bastard is big and hurts!" Although I pity him, I have to laugh. "That's what they call irony of fate." I understand his indignation. It doesn't light up his mood as I nominate Saint James as prime suspect to have punished him with the blister for yesterday's revelry.

But his mood changes as we arrive at San Marco, a village just a few meters away from Monte do Gozo. Thomas takes a look at his watch, does a little exercise test with the blistered foot and waves good-bye. "I need a bathtub, a comfortable bed and maybe a nice massage. So I'll see you tomorrow in Santiago!" I could walk the last few kilometres too, but I am not ready to quit my first Camino right here and now. I salute Thomas. "When I arrive tomorrow morning, my dear prophet, I expect a donkey at the city boundary, palm leaf-waving virgins all along the way till the cathedral and of course a choir singing Hallelujah!" He grabs his phone and pretends to call a psychiatrist. "Hello Dr. Rosenberg? Yes, now he became absolutely nuts. Yes, yes… bonkers as a mad weasel. What? Wait a moment….beer transfusion, a knock on the head and some kind of tribal dance?… Alright, thank you doc!" I shrug. "Ok, compromise: they must not be virgins. See you tomorrow!"

Monte do Gozo is enormous. The way the complex of buildings looks, it seems to have been constructed by some fascistic architects in the late 60's as a recreation boot camp for the fascist youth of Generalissimo Franco's

Spain. Like Lego bricks, block by block are in a row along some kind of alley, leading to a large square where a bar, a laundry and a restaurant are situated. They have been very generous with space here. In my mind I can see young men in black uniforms marching along the alley. It is almost as spacious as the area of Nuremberg rally. It is only consequent, not to say congruent, that the albergue inside is constructed in a very logical way too. Very straight and proper. I come to know that this Albergue has been built in 1993 on the occasion of the holy year and the visit of Pope John Paul II. Well, my error was, due to the architecture, quite obvious. Dear Spaniards, we need to talk about your taste of design!

Mustafa, Claudio, Ib and the girls have already arrived. The two Austrian women that we've met twice already on The Way, are sitting on a wall, enjoying the afternoon sun. They wave at me. This time I resign to wind them up.

I check into a six-bed dormitory and the miasma of stinking boots at the entrance to the room hits my nostrils. This is incredible. I feel as if have I have stepped into the cage of a very old lion suffering from incontinence, digesting the decomposing remains of a two-week dead skunk. Or in other words, it smells like the boys' locker room at high school shortly before summer holidays. Some people are too dopey to notice and use the boot-shelf outside of the rooms. What are those people doing to their feet? Do they let them decay? I behave snooty on purpose and grab my dirty clothes. While they take a short vacation at the laundry, I enjoy a long and hot shower. Claudio and company are already having an early dinner at the "bar and tienda de la calle" at San Marco. I order a bocadillo and a glass of white wine and enjoy the evening sun on the porch of the tienda. Close to me sits a strawberry-blonde belle and her mum. Her name is Caris, and she reminds me a bit of an adult version of Peppermint Patty. She and her mom have already arrived at noon. They are pleasant company but I am not in the mood to make new friends, so our talk is just skin deep, but admittedly convenient. In the backlight I see the French guy with the Ukulele appear. He is followed by a thin, limping dog. Ukulele takes a seat and rolls himself a cigarette. "The dog is following me now for more than 35 kilometres." The owner of the tienda knows the dog. "That's one of those Camino dogs, walking the way forth and back and choosing part-time humans for a while. Too wild to be tamed and too domesticated to be independent." The poor little thing is exhausted, so I get

him some water and some ham. As we are sitting there, we do what we have done most of the evenings. We share stories. Three German girls take a seat close to us. They just arrived from the Camino Del Norte, which they started at Oviedo, walking along the coast. Everybody who is sitting there is satisfied and relaxed to the core. And all of us are in anticipation of our arrival at the Praca do Obradoiro tomorrow morning. Like me, the three Germans want to walk into Santiago with the rising sun. Caris lets her glance stray around and suddenly murmurs: "Tomorrow…" I can understand her, but that's a bit too stagy. So I start to sing a gentle "Tomorrow" from the musical Annie. "Tomorrow! Tomorrow! I love yah, tomorrow! You're always a day away!"
I earn an evil eye followed by a forgiving smile. Sometimes I can be such a charming little devil!
As I walk back to the Albergue, I pass the large monument that has been erected on the highest point of Monte do Gozo. So shortly before dusk it appears grand, but there is a likeness to the sculptures which are meant to impress, that are so popular in dictatorships. Well, not such a big difference between dictatorships and religions, the heretic thought comes to my mind. The night is clear, no cloud to be seen; tomorrow is not

only a day away, tomorrow is going to be a lovely day. And so one earworm is replaced by another. Bill Withers is much better for a lullaby.

Some facts about the stage Arzua – Monte do Gozo:

Length: 35 km, Duration: 9 hours
Altitude difference: short before Monte do Gozo 100 meters ascend.
Breakpoints: Santa Irene; Ruá, Pedrouzo/Arca, Lavacolla, Villamayor, San Marcos.
Until Monte do Gozo the only mentionable Albergues are to be found in Pedrouzo, before and after some smaller rural hostels and hotels.
Infrastructure: enough bars and restaurants along the way, nice little bar and tienda at San Marcos, which is the official name of the village on the Monte do Gozo.
The albergue Monte do Gozo is of a gargantuan size. It includes beside many beds a restaurant, a laundry and an ATM.
Places of interest: The way leads you through eucalyptus forests where the air smells fresh and healthy. As soon as you have reached the periphery of Santiago Airport you will cross a small creek. This

place is called Lavacolla where in early times the pilgrims used to wash off the dirt of their pilgrimage before entering Santiago. The Monte do Gozo at the village San Marco is the place where the towers of the cathedral could be seen for the first time. The Pilgrim, noticing the cathedral first was allowed to carry the title "King of the pilgrims"- "el rey de los peregrinos". Many European family names like "Rey, Roy, Leroi or König" are based on this tradition. Tip: If you stay at Monte do Gozo you have the chance to walk to Santiago in the early morning hours, when everything is still calm and quiet. The atmosphere on the Praca de Obradoiro at sunrise is very special.

Walking diary
Santiago de Compostela,   May, 23, 2012

BeepBeepBeep! 5:30 in the morning. The alarm of my cell phone rings. Too bad that it falls down from the upper bunk bed and vanishes under the lower bed. It takes a few minutes until I find it. Tadah! On my last day I made it. I woke up a complete dormitory and made everybody hate me. The late riser strikes back. The Revenge of The Dude. Yes, that could be a great film title. My backpack is ready, I inhale a fast espresso from a coffee vending machine and I am ready to walk. It is 06.00 o´ clock as I leave the Albergue. Jihae and Tracy pass by giggling; they want to see the sunrise from Monte do Gozos Monument. I wave at them: "See you in Santiago!" Ib, the Dane, is ready to walk too, so we walk together the last five kilometres of the long journey. The sunrise is not as sensational as we hoped for, but it's a beautiful day. For two kilometres, we cross the suburban area of Santiago. The first street signs that announce the cathedral and the historic centre are to be seen. The yellow arrows and scallops that have been familiar markers on the way have vanished as a fading memory. The modern buildings lose ground to the architecture of the middle-age. On the right hand we pass an ancient and beautiful building, which is part of the University of Santiago. We step through an archway and have arrived. We are standing on the Praca do Obradoiro. The impressive towers of the minster are doused in a golden morning light. It is short past seven. We are all alone on the large plaza. Well, no virgins, no palm leafs, no Hosannas, not even a donkey, but a wonderful, silent reception. The pilgrims' office opens its gates at 09.00h. We have lots of time for breakfast. The three German girls from yesterday have arrived too, so we search together for the next bar. A few alleys away we discover a neat little bar that just opened its doors. The smell of fresh bakery-delivered croissants is awesome. A glass of champagne would be fine, but they serve only white wine. It doesn't matter. My brain is drowning in endorphins and an indescribable happiness fulfills me. It's a delicate sensation and this feeling is going to remain the whole day. The girls and Ib feel the same; there is a smile inside of us that perhaps can be compared with the glow on the faces of a young love. Filled with wonder, like Juliet on her balcony, listening to the sweet words of Romeo, we notice this rare and delicate smile on the faces of almost all arriving pilgrims during the day. Shortly before 9:00 a.m., we are sitting opposite of the pilgrims' office and wait for the door to be opened. As it does, the queue of pilgrims grows fast. After a short waiting period I finally receive my Compostela that certifies that I have walked from Leon to Santiago as a pilgrim on my own feet. That they have misspelled my Christian name doesn't bother me. I take it as a sign not to become coltish and not to overrate my personal success.

With the Compostela in my hand, I step on the Ruá do Vilar. I look around in research of a nice little hotel. For the moment I am

131

done with dormitories and bunk beds. I have a necessity for a soft bed, cool linen sheets and a cozy pillow. Someone pulls me backwards on my backpack. "Hey pilgrim!" Thomas beams at me. "Have you been canonized?" We agree to meet around noon at the cathedral. Around the corner, at the Plaza de Fonseca, I discover the Hotel Brabantes Libradon. It is small, neat and offers me a nice single room for just 45.- Euros. The hotels situation is fantastic. In the middle of the historic centre, only a stone's throw away from the cathedral and the pilgrims' office. The courteous lady at the reception shows me the way to the next Zara store. Fresh, clean and fashionable clothes are exactly what I need right now. One hour later, back in my room, I can dress myself, well-groomed and perfumed, in mint green chinos and a pale blue collarless shirt. After two weeks of more useful clothing, I'm in need of a flash of color. My feet are overjoyed cause of the pair of espadrilles I bought them. As I look into the mirror I notice that I lost weight. No more love handles. "Dammit Janet" I murmur to myself. "You are a handsome little devil!" Of course this is self-mockery. I swear. I bounce down the stairs, step on the alley and linger towards the cathedral. I am quite early so I look around to see who's already there. I discover Mustafa, who applauds me for my new appearance and asks for the way to the Zara store. The sound of the mighty bells calls the pilgrims, faithful or not, to the service. I step into the cathedral too; my pilgrimage is not finished yet. One thing is still missing; I have to hug the statue of Saint James, a ritual that is part of the whole pilgrimage. The dome is filled to the last seat. I can't remember having seen such a crowded church in my entire life. I look around and discover many familiar faces; a silent wave is how we greet for the moment. There is Donna, Katharina, the two Austrian mountain goats, Claudio, a couple from Cologne, James and Carol, Eva, Hannah, Jihae and Tracy, sunken in her prayer. In a marble covered alcove I come to rest, and let the scenery act upon me.

I think of my dad and how much I would love to tell him about this experience of mine. He always was the one I could talk best with about with my latest discovery, experience or perception. I light a candle for him. Tears come to my eyes and quietly I leave the cathedral. Outside, under a bright blue sky, I reflect upon my feelings. I am proud and grateful for what I experienced. I am simultaneously exhilarated while being extremely relaxed.

Wide awake, super attentive and surfing on the wave of a very colorful inner light, I take a seat close to Thomas who is sitting outside of a bar close to the plaza. With him are the two Austrian barflies that knocked him out 2 days ago. We chat while savoring the scenery and a glass of Rioja. During the day we meet and see many other faces from the way.

In the early evening hours, we sit opposite of my hotel at the Praca Fonseca and enjoy the other people around us. The three German girls that I had breakfast with are there, and so are Daddy Müller from Neuschwanstein with his sons too. They wave at us, so we join them. "Hey guys! So…any plans for tonight?" Tom and I are in consensus. "Fiesta!" Glasses tingle, cold beer refreshes thirsty throats and Thomas quotes AC/DC in a Santiago way: "For those about to walk …. We salute you!" "What a pity the Helmut isn't here with us!" he says. "And? Was it what you expected?"

I reflect. "Well, the only expectation I had was to have a new experience. And this expectation has definitely been fulfilled. But if you ask me how I felt in the last 12 days…well…it had had everything a perfect journey needs!" A Dutch peregrina with shiny ginger hair, sitting close to me, interferes "And what is that for you? A perfect journey?" "Oh, that's easy. A good mix of new impressions, beautiful landscapes, new friends, likable people, good conversations, the possibility to reflect on oneself and last, not least, a lot of fun." She nods. "Fun is good, but it is not everything, especially on the Camino." I agree. "Call it how you like to; fun, Lust for life, joy, happiness, whatever. Without joy, laughter and a little bit of goofiness even tons of reflection, meditation and contemplation are not worth a dime." She laughs and Thomas says the closing rate: "Salute, let's celebrate!"

The cathedral in the early morning hours

Some facts about the last few miles to Santiago and some useful information:

Length: 5 km, Duration: 1 hour
The suburbs of Santiago are, like every other town in the universe, negligible.
Through the Porta do Camino we step and reach the Praca do Cervantes, named after the famous author of Don Quixote, the man from La Mancha.
From now on Santiago offers its middle age charm and beauty. We cross the Praca Inmaculada on the northern side of the cathedral, where the traditional entrance for the pilgrims is to be found. (Well, nowadays

136

most people don't know anymore about this tradition.) Through an arcade we step from the shades into the light out on the Praca do Obradoiro, where the magnificent western front of the cathedral, that has been finished in the middle of the 18th century, awaits us. The origins of the glorious building are from the 9th century. The oldest still existing part is the Romanesque church inside the dome from the 11th century. Standing in front of the main entrance we can see the luxurious Parador Hotel to our left, which has been erected in 1509 as a hostel and hospital for the pilgrims by order from the king and queen of Spain. There is still a rule that says that the first 10 pilgrims of the day which ask for food at the hotels backdoor will be fed for free. Pilgrims receive a discount of 15% at the hotel for the night and 10% for food and beverages.

When turning to the right and then, short before the Praca Fonseca, to the left, the second street on the right is the Ruá do Vilar, where the Pilgrims Office is situated on the left in opposite of the hotel Rua Villar and its terrace.

Infrastructure: There are hundreds of small hostels, hotels, inns and Albergues, innumerable bars and restaurants. I can recommend by own experience the hotels

Rua Villar (Ruá do Villar) and the Hotel Brabantes Libradon (Praca Fonseca). Need some fresh clothes? Ask the receptionist of your hotel or at the tourists' office (100 meters away from the pilgrims' office) for the way to the next Zara store or department store.

You can get a street map there for free too. The Pilgrims Office opens at 09.00. Here you will receive the reward for your struggle: The Compostela. At the office you can receive information about church services, the cathedral, Saint James and pilgrim events too.

Places of interest:

Santiago itself: Santiago de Compostela is not only the third important place of pilgrimage for the Christianity after Jerusalem and Rome. It is a lively, vivid and agile university town, where history and modernity walk hand in hand. The origins of Santiago go back to the Romans in the 1st century. In the 11th century Santiago became the famous pilgrims' place it is since then. The university, founded in 1501, has a long and important history as well. The cathedral: If you arrive early try to visit the cathedral as early as possible if you want to hug Saint James or enjoy the dome in silence. From early noon on the cathedral will be crowded by hundreds of pilgrims and *thousands of tourists and cruise ship passengers.*

The pilgrims mass is held at noon. On Fridays, holidays or if someone has been generous, the large censer, called botafumeiro, will be swung through the central aisle. The first (and mostly more meditative) church service of the day is held in Spanish at 07.30 daily.

Special tip: the cathedrals museum is worth a visit, especially the walk on the roofs of the cathedral! Tickets are available at the museum.

Walk the town and enjoy getting lost on the middle age alleys, sit somewhere and watch the people passing by, take a rest in the shades of an arcade or a churches side aisle instead of following a guide. Don't be afraid to feel guilty because you have not seen this or that tourist feature. It does not matter. You did something great. The things you have seen and experienced on the way are incomparable. Relax, have a good time, enjoy the town.

Remember: You are stardust.

Diary
Santiago de Compostela,   May, 24, 2012

I wake up at 10.00 in the morning. Last
night we celebrated, talked, danced and had
a good time until three. I have to check out
at noon, but I can leave my backpack at the
reception. After breakfast we take a seat on
the terrace of the bar opposite the pilgrims'
office. We hope for familiar faces to arrive.
Eleven - thirty seems to be a perfect time for
a first glass of white wine. One of Daddy
Müllers sons joins us. As a real
Neuschwansteinian, he orders a beer. The
eighty-year-old rambler with the bushy
beard walks along the Ruá do Vilar and
greets us by waving with his gnarly walking
stick. And then we see Karen stepping out of
the pilgrims' office. We both jump up.
"Karen!" We wave at her, she smiles all
over her face and is as pleased as we are. We
sit together for more than an hour and talk
about our adventures before Karen leaves to
search for a hotel. Two hours time until I
have to move to the airport.
The man in his late fifties with the grey
beard, who stands close to me, is a guy I
helped yesterday morning with a few
painkillers cause of his limping."Hey, how
are you? By the way, thanks one more time
for the Ibu´s." "Hey! So, feeling better?

140

How are your feet? Take a seat." He is one of the coy, modest guys, not the type of person that is flamboyant, but he has an aura of sangfroid and calmness. An aplomb one only receives when one has survived some troubles in life. We have a wine together and although I did not ask him, he tells me his reason to walk the way. Two years ago, he won a hard struggle against cancer, he is not yet sure if a relapse can be excluded. "But!" he says "I swore an oath to myself then, that if I get out of that alive, I will walk the way to Santiago. And if it is the last thing I can do." "And now?" I ask him. "Now? I'm feeling better than ever. If I don't have the power to survive further deep hits by now, then I'll never have it." He laughs deep from his heart and I feel with him. He takes the last sip of his glass and bids us farewell. "Bye boys! Buen Camino, where ever you may be!"

We decide to change places and as we walk towards the small bar below the cathedral, we meet Alberto from Brazil. He is going to leave tomorrow on a plane to Rio. So we are sitting there in a threesome, talking, laughing and drinking a last glass of wine together until we get more and more reflective.

As I leave to get my backpack from the reception of the hotel, I have a last touching adventure. While I am waiting for the receptionist to finish her phone call, I notice a very cultivated and attractive Spanish lady. She is looking around in the small lobby in a way that shows a bit of confusion. I can tell by the way she gazes, that she just has arrived from her way. I can barely judge her age. She could be in her early forties as well as in her late fifties. She is a woman of that hard to find and rare timeless beauty. I smile at her. "I can recommend this place." She smiles too and the expression on her face still shows the emotion of having arrived and the emotion about the experiences she made on her way. Her eyes are shining; they beam like a sapphire laser. "Thank you so much! How was the way for you?" Such a personal question from a total stranger, here and now, does not alienate me. I feel somehow connected to her; and a little bit attracted too. "It was fantastic, the whole thing, the people, the experiences, the landscape, my own thoughts and… situations like this one…it was, it is…overwhelming." She nods and in a fast sequence she gives me a Siamese, a knowing and a rapt smile. "Yes, that's the way I feel too." Then she embraces me and kisses me twice on my cheeks, after a blink of an eye her lips touch mine in a gentle but very sensual way for a short but exquisite moment.

"Buen viaje, guapo y Buen Camino!"

I take my backpack, step out on the street of medieval cobblestones and I smile.

Arrival at 07.00

The 100 kilometer stone – and a Dude

At noon at the Praca do Obradoiro

145

Some useful vocabulary

Don't worry if you babble gibberish. A bit pidgin is always better than no Spanish at all! Give it a try!

Hola!	Hallo!
Buenos dias	good day
Buenas tardes	good afternoon
Buenas noches	good evening/night
Que tal?	How are you?
Bien	good
Todo va bien	everything is fine
Peregrino	Pilgrim
Oficina de peregrinos	Pilgrims office
(Yo) no/soy	I am/not
(Yo) no/tengo	I /don't /have
Necesito	I need
Quiero (key:air:o)	I want/I like to
Quieremos	We want/ we like to
No quiero	I don't want
Tienes? (tea:ey:ness)	Do you have…?
Donde es?	Where is?
Por favor	Please!
(Muchas) Gracias	Thanks! (a lot)
Atencion!	Attention!
Soccoro!	Help!
Vale!	OK!
Vamos!	Let´s go!
Perdon	Sorry / excuse me!
Lo siento	I am very sorry

Hasta pronto	See you soon
Hasta luego	See you later
Adios	Good bye
Hasta mañana	See you tomorrow
Señor/Señora/Señorita	Sir/Madam/Miss
(The ñ is pronounced like nj (San:Yo:ra)	
La cama	The bed
La litera	The bunk bed
Arriba	Above
Abajo	below
Nombre	Name
con/sin	with/without
Aqua con/sin gas	sparkling
water/plain water	
Cerveza (sir:wee:zer)	Beer
sin alcohol	without alcohol
Vino tinto	Red wine
Vino blanco	White wine
Botella	Bottle
Vaso/Copa	Glas
Carta	Menu
Menu peregrino	Pilgrims meal
Desayuno	Breakfast
Comida	Lunch
Cena	Dinner
Pagar	(to) pay
La Cuenta	the bill
Bocadillo	Sub-Sandwich
Azucar	Sugar
Jamon	Ham
Huevo	Egg

Helado	Ice cream
Hielo	Ice cube
Pan	Bread
Queso (Ke:so)	Cheese
Croquettas	(ham) croquette
Patatas fritas	French fries
Tortilla	Omelette
Atun	Tuna
Empanada	Samosa
Aceituna (R:say:tuna)	Olive
Limon	Lemon
Manzana	Apple
Platano	Banana
Naranja	Orange
Ajo	Garlic
Sed	Thirst
Hambre	Hunger
Cigarillo	Cigarette
Fumar	Smoking
Cenicero	Ashtray
Farmacia	Pharmacy
Medico	Doctor
Dolor	Pain
Diarrea	Diarrhea
Aqua (non) potable	(not) drinkable water
Flecha amarillo	yellow arrow

Some (simplified) phrases as examples

Hola! Mi nombre es…
Hi! My name is…

Donde es…(una albergue) ?
Where is…(a hostel)?

Hola! Buenas tardes, senor. Que tal?
Hallo, good afternoon, sir. How are you?

Tengo sed. Quiéro una cerveza sin alcohol por favor.
I am thirsty. I´d like a beer without alcohol please.

Por favor, quiero una comida. Tienes una carta?
Please, I´d like to eat something. Do you have a menu?

Buenas tardes. Quieremos dos camas. Con preferencia en arriba. Gracias!
Good afternoon, we like to have two beds. Preferably the upper one. Thank you!

149

The flight of the stork

Tom, Karen and me at Fonfria